WELL-FOUNDED HOPE

WELL-FOUNDED
HOPE

Hendrikus Berkhof

JOHN KNOX PRESS
Richmond, Virginia

Standard Book Number: 8042–0460–8
Library of Congress Catalog Card Number: 69-13272
© M. E. Bratcher 1969
Printed in the United States of America

To the University of Aberdeen
in gratitude for
the degree of Doctor of Divinity

Preface

This book is the result of an invitation extended to me by the Austin Presbyterian Theological Seminary to deliver the Westervelt lectures of 1967. I gladly accepted the opportunity to see a well-known seminary where many Dutch theological students spent an unforgettable year, to visit my daughter who that year was such a student, and—last but not least—to formulate and compose some thoughts on eschatology which were waiting in my mind for the appropriate moment. The limits of the lectures urged me to avoid digressions and to concentrate on fundamental questions. In spite of having to leave out so many aspects and problems, I see this limitation more as a gain than as a loss, because unlike former generations, our contemporaries are less interested in all kinds of details than in the question, On what ground and to what extent are statements about the future possible? And this is the question which underlies these lectures.

I delivered them to an audience of theological students and ministers but from the beginning meant them also for interested laymen. If theology is a function of the whole church on its way through the world, theologians are not allowed to write in such a way that they are understood only by a small group of specialists. In view of this wider circle I added afterwards a chapter on "Eschatology and Futurology," a problem which is very timely but towards which we have made only the first steps.

On the other hand I wanted to stimulate my theological readers to a broader and deeper study of the subject. I tried to do so partly by the annotations which I made and partly by the addition of the closing chapter, which I originally wrote for a Dutch theological magazine and which is meant to function in this book as a kind of theological background to the previous chapters. This is the only chapter written for "specialists." The reader who leaves it out is at no disadvantage in understanding the other chapters.

As a foreigner I have a very limited active English vocabulary. I wish to thank the editors of John Knox Press, who helped me to better formulations than I could invent myself. I hope that the message which this book tries to transmit is understandable to everyone who shares in the Christian hope.

H. BERKHOF

Leiden University
The Netherlands
February, 1968

Contents

I

The Crisis of
the Christian Expectation
of the Future

There is ample reason to speak of a crisis in the Christian expectation of the future. The preaching of Jesus was full of the future; Paul and the other New Testament writers were radically oriented towards the future because they knew that in Christ that future had already begun. Nowadays things look completely different in the vast majority of the Christian churches. Our minds are not full of the great future; in fact, it often plays hardly more than a vague role. Of course, we can blame ourselves and each other, but that does not bring us any further. We do better to ask first of all, Why does the Christian expectation of the future mean so little to us?

Our churches usually impress upon us that which is in agreement with the Apostles' Creed, according to which we believe in four elements, four successive phases: first, the Second Coming of Christ; second, the resurrection of the dead; then, Christ's judgment of the quick and the dead; and finally, life everlasting, either as salvation or as rejection. One going deeper into these subjects is supposed to believe that this world shall be changed in the twinkling of an eye at the last trumpet; that the graves shall be opened; that Christ on his judgment throne will open the books; and that when the last judgment is over, the holy city, new Jerusalem, all finished will descend to earth.

Very little about this, however, is heard in sermons and in Sunday schools. Evidently this expectation of the future embarrasses both ministers and church members. Why? Because we consider this representation of the matter utterly obsolete, whether or

not we are aware of doing so. We happen to live and breathe in a
world of endless space and time, the product of an evolution of
many millions of years, which is ruled to its farthest corners by the
same laws. There is no room for either heaven or hell and even less
for somebody who would be descending from heaven to earth on
a cloud. And we cannot believe in a sudden, complete change, an
invasion from above which would violently destroy the agelong
evolution. That is why more and more people, when these things
are discussed, say, "But all that is, of course, imagery." I agree. But
such a magic word does not solve the problem. We have to continue
asking, "Imagery of what, exactly?" and "Is that which is really
meant, credible for us?" As long as we do not ask and answer these
questions, both believers and nonbelievers will keep thinking that
a person who is called a Christian has to hold a very fantastic and
mythological expectation concerning the future.

Under such circumstances we may be grateful for theologians
who try to express the Christian expectation of the future in language both understandable and inspiring for us. Since the First
World War many have been at work on this. It is no use to enumer-
ate their names here. I mention only Rudolf Bultmann as the interpreter of a specific concept of future, i.e., the existential one, which
exercised a tremendous influence after World War II. What he and
his followers understand by expectation of the future might be
described as follows:

The essence of man lies in his "existing." This means literally
to step outside one's self. All the terrestrial realities are elements
confined in themselves and objects of the existing world. Man, too,
is such an element. But at the same time, he is much more. He can
step outside himself, he can project himself towards the future; this
makes him a subject in the midst of the world of objects; by that
he is no longer a slave but free—not only thrown into the world but
also withdrawing himself from the world, projecting himself towards the future, grasping for the "reality of his existence."

Is man capable of doing this on his own accord? Philosophers
such as Heidegger and Sartre preach that he is. But Bultmann
denies it. Man is unable to pull himself out of the swamp. He has
to grasp the hand which God holds out. That hand is the preaching

of the crucified Christ, through whom man is called to faith and discipleship. This is the power which enables us to come out of our fallen state in the world to real freedom, to authentic existence. In preaching we are confronted with the "last things," the eschaton, the future, i.e., that which comes to us from God—the gift of a true existence. Many New Testament writers have expressed this experience in mythological terms in speaking of a miraculous future, either close-at-hand or more distant, toward which we are bound. According to Bultmann both Paul and John knew better. For them eternity was here and now, since we have died and were raised with Christ and have passed from death to life. More specifically one can think of Romans 6 and John 5. In the latter chapter (vss. 24 f.) it is said: "Truly, truly, I say to you, he who hears my word and believes him who sent me, has eternal life; he does not come into judgment, but has passed from death to life. Truly, truly, I say to you, the hour is coming, and now is, when the dead will hear the voice of the Son of God, and those who hear will live." So it is in the proclamation here and now that we experience the future.[1] The future is not a cosmic event bound to happen within a certain time. It is our existential freedom, which is not at our disposal but which is ever before us as an invitation of God and towards which we have to project ourselves ever anew.

This modern existential interpretation of the biblical expectation of the future has fascinated many, especially in the period 1950-1960. At the moment, this fascination has decreased considerably. There are at least two causes. The first is that the elements of time and of progress in time not only are mythical wordings but belong to the essence of the matter and therefore cannot be eliminated from the biblical expectation of the future. The second reason is that this presentation appealed to people right after the war when the shock of the war was still strong. The existentialist escape from the horizontal world has given way to a new improvement idealism, a willingness to fight for a better world of real liberty, equality, and fraternity. Natural science and sociology have made the world predictable. We know how we shall progress and how much progress we shall make in this respect in the next decades unless a war breaks out. As in the Middle Ages people were thrilled by a tremendous expectation of the future as they approached the year 1000, so we are now as we approach the year 2000—with the difference that the pious people in the Middle Ages expected the kingdom of God from heaven, whereas our generation looks forward to the kingdom of man as the fruit of technical science and planning. And this contrast leads us to our question: Can the biblical expectation of the future be expressed in language understandable and inspiring, not for the existentialists of yesterday but for the "futurists" of today and tomorrow?

It is a fact that beside an existentialistic theology, a futuristic one is also developing today. As in the former there was hardly room for the concept of future, so in the latter that concept is all and everything. And just as the former was influenced by Heidegger and Sartre, so the futuristic theology is inspired by the philosopher Ernst Bloch, a Jewish Marxist thinker who after his break with communism fled from Eastern to Western Germany. For Bloch the essence of man's being lies not in an existence here and now but in our being on the way to the future—not in what we have but in what we expect or rather in the very fact of expecting, in our looking forward to that which does not yet have a name or a place. Something that does not yet have a name or a place is in Greek called *ou-topos*, our word "utopia." Bloch calls himself a utopian thinker. Being a Jew, he relies heavily on the Old Testament, particularly Moses and his "God of the Exodus," who called himself "I will be with you as I will be with you." (See Exodus 3:14.)

Though Bloch thinks that we do not need a faith in God any longer to justify our being directed towards the future, it is no wonder that he fascinated talented younger theologians in Germany and elsewhere. Especially Jürgen Moltmann's book *Theology of Hope* has become very well-known. Moltmann wants to show again the eschatological character of the Christian faith in all its aspects and to put it into words for modern man. According to him God is not yet really present in this world. His presence is the great future toward which we are bound. The word of God in the Old Testament, the coming of Christ, and particularly his resurrection are signposts to this unknown future, placed by God in this world.

Man is a being-on-his-way; faith is hope; the believer, a fighter for change; the church, an "exodus community": we live on the *promissio*, which means both "promise" and "being sent forward."

Moltmann's book has had one printing after another and has reduced considerably the influence of Bultmann's "eternity here and now." And rightly so, insofar as it expresses far more clearly the biblical witness about the future than does the concept of existentialism. Yet I do not think that we can uncritically choose this futurism over against existentialism. Both get stuck in a very formal concept of eschatology. For Bultmann it is the invitation to existence which comes to us in the present. For Moltmann the future which beckons us has hardly any substance. The principle hope (see the title of Bloch's main work) is more important than what is hoped for. At the same time both theologians live on each other's shortcomings. For Bultmann the eschaton is entirely today; for Moltmann, entirely future. In all this the latter is less one-sided than Bultmann, since he does not deny—later he even expressed himself more strongly in this respect—that we do not know this future apart from the present and the past, particularly not apart from the resurrection of Christ.[2]

Existentialism on the one hand and futurism on the other are, so to speak, the buoys which mark the clear channel for us. But are we really able to say something more than those two concepts do? Can we really know anything about the future without falling into fantasy and mythology—anything understandable and inspiring for our time, for us who live so much by the tangible and verifiable? It seems to me that we may answer this question affirmatively; but before we can do that, we first have to deal with the method of the expectation of the future.

II

The Method of
the Christian Expectation
of the Future

The word "method" comes from the Greek *methodos*, "access." We face the question, How do we gain access to the world of the future, which is closed for us? On what basis and with what authority can we ever make reliable statements about anything as uncertain as the future?

Let us first see whether we can find out how the Old Testament and New Testament witnesses approached the future. It has often been asserted that Israel's expectation of the future was the result of the grim times before and during the exile. In that case the expectation of the kingdom of God and his victory would have been the result of despair about defeat in the present. This faith would then have been a kind of projection, a self-made consolation. Marx and Freud would then be right with their presentation of faith as an illusion. In fact, Israel's expectation of the future must have been much older. It must have already existed in the hearts of the patriarchs, whom we have to imagine as so-called half-nomads who were looking forward to the time that their race could settle down in the fertile land. This same expectation must also have inspired the tribes who wandered in the Sinai peninsula. But after entry into the land this direction towards the future did not disappear; it took the shape of confidence that what God was giving in this land and this state would be continued and completed. A very important element in this expectation became the promise which, according to 2 Samuel 7, the prophet Nathan transmitted to King David: ". . . the LORD will make you a house. . . . I will raise up your offspring . . . and I will establish his kingdom. I will be his father, and he shall be my son." And David's answer: "What other nation on earth is like thy people Israel, whom God went to redeem to be his people . . . And thou didst establish for thyself thy people Israel to be thy people for ever; and thou, O LORD, didst become their God" (vss. 11 f., 14, 23 f.). David sees this promise for his posterity as the confirmation of God's faithfulness which he had shown in history to his elected people. The future is the continuation, confirmation, extension, and fulfillment of what God has accomplished in the past and the present.

This promise, which in the broader sense of this word we call "messianic," was deepened and changed in subsequent times. The prophets showed the people in times of apostasy and in times of distress how little self-evident and how undeserved this promise was and how it could only find its fulfillment through judgment. But need itself did not create this expectation. When the people, even in the deepest darkness, clung to this expectation, it was because of the experiences which they had gained with their God in history. These experiences were concentrated around David's kingship. ". . . and I will make with you an everlasting covenant, [according to] my steadfast, sure love for David" (Isa. 55:3). But even more they were concentrated around the moment of Israel's birth. David also fell back on this event when he said that in the great acts of exodus and entry, God had liberated his people from the peoples and their gods. Time and again the prophets return to this event as the pledge of the expectation of the future; for this future they even frequently use pictures derived from the miracles of the exodus. For example, "Thus says the LORD, who makes a way in the sea, a path in the mighty waters . . . I will make a way in the wilderness and rivers in the desert . . . to give drink to my chosen people, the people whom I formed for myself that they might declare my praise" (Isa. 43:16, 19 ff.).[1]

Faithful Israel had access to the unknown future because it knew about past and present and believed in the faithfulness of its God. We may say that the eschatology of Israel is the confession of God's faithfulness projected on the screen of the future. Or, with the words of Vriezen, "The basis of all expectations of salvation is faith in Yahweh, i.e. *He who is*, faith in the actual presence of the

Holy God, who is also the God of salvation . . . This promise with respect to the future lies in the actuality of Yahweh and in His covenant-relationship with His people . . . This security remains the basis of all further relationships, even of the most contradictory hopes."[2]

Let us now turn to the New Testament. Here we find the same method, the same *methodos* or access road in making statements about the future. Here also these statements have as a basis that which happened in the past. The difference from the Old Testament is that there the basic facts are God's acts of salvation in exodus and entry and in the kingship of David; whereas for the New Testament witnesses the coming, the work, the death and resurrection of Jesus Christ, and the descent of the Holy Spirit are central. Therefore, the future is viewed here as a repetition and continuation on a world-wide scale of what in these events has come to light about God's salvation on the one hand and man's resistance on the other. Hence, the expectation of the future contains both the coming of the antichrist and the coming of Christ in glory.

More recent eschatological literature has rightly pointed out that in the New Testament the future is seen as an unfolding of what is given in the resurrection of Christ. However, little or no attention has been paid to the fact that the eschaton is also seen as the unfolding and completion of what the Spirit already works here and now in the hearts and lives of people. The risen Lord is called "first fruits" of the harvest of the future, but this is also the name for the Spirit. And the Spirit is even referred to as "guarantee," "pledge," "earnest money," or "down payment" of the great future —terms taken from the commercial world.[3] Sometimes the future is seen as completion of what has begun in Christ, sometimes as completion of what the Spirit has begun, and sometimes as comple-tion of both—of the double event of Christ's resurrection and of the work of renewal which the Spirit has begun. Let us look at an example of each of these.

The Christological foundation of the future is found particularly in 1 Corinthians 15, where Paul sketches the coming resurrection as a consequence of and analogy to Christ's resurrection. "Now if

Christ is preached as raised from the dead, how can some of you say that there is no resurrection of the dead? . . . But in fact Christ has been raised from the dead, the first fruits of those who have fallen asleep" (vss. 12, 20).[4]

We find the foundation of the future in the work of the Spirit powerfully described in Romans 5. There Paul speaks of the hope and says, ". . . hope does not disappoint us, because God's love has been poured into our hearts through the Holy Spirit which has been given to us" (vs. 5). This love is so new and so overwhelming, that it assures the believer that one day all of reality will be transformed in the style of this love.[5]

In 1 Peter 1:3 the future is founded in both the resurrection of Christ and the work of the Spirit: "Blessed be the God and Father of our Lord Jesus Christ! By his great mercy we have been born anew to a living hope through the resurrection of Jesus Christ from the dead." So it is one continuous process; the new life of Jesus Christ leads through the Spirit to a new life for people who, on account of his resurrection and in virtue of their being born again, take courage to believe in a future which will be an extension of those two miracles and which will at the same time surpass them.[6]

In short, in the New Testament the future is the unfolding and completion of that which already exists in Christ and the Spirit and which will be carried through triumphantly in spite of sin, suffering, and death.[7]

We find this conviction also in a surprising way in the terminology which the New Testament writers use to describe the future. All these terms are used—although usually by other writers —to indicate the first coming and work of Christ or the working of the Holy Spirit. Every Bible reader can confirm that with the help of a concordance. *Life everlasting* points mainly to the future, but especially in John it means also the life which is already present in faith in Christ. *Revelation* (the two Greek words are *apokalupsis* and *epiphaneia*) took place in Christ, is given to us by the Spirit, and is expected from the future. The *day* is the day of Christ's appearance but also the day of salvation which is now by virtue of the Spirit, and especially the great day of the coming judgment. The *hour* or *time* (Greek: *kairos*) is in the first place the hour of the Son of Man, the time which has been fulfilled but also the hour in which the Spirit awakens us, the "time of His pleasure," and "the fullness of time" to which we are looking forward. The *judgment* is that for which Christ came into the world, which the Spirit continues in the church and the world, and which one day will be fully executed. Finally the well-known word "parousia," which simply means "presence" or "coming," is used mostly for the great future but also for the earthly life of Jesus (2 Peter 1:16).

It is also significant how certain Old Testament prophecies are related to the future in one place in the New Testament and in another place are considered as being fulfilled in Christ's first coming.[8] All this confirms what has been said previously: The people who write here had access to the future on the basis of their experience with God in past and present. For them the future had begun already. This was not because they could count on an automatic continuation of certain developments but because of God, who is faithful; because of Christ, who is the same yesterday, today, and forever; and because of the Spirit, who will continue to the end the work that he has begun.

As a consequence of all this we now see that Christian hope in its nature and structure differs widely from what in common parlance we call hope. When, according to the Greek saga, Pandora in disobedience opened the box with which she was entrusted, all the diseases and disasters flew away; only hope stayed inside. That is the ineradicable human passion for life, which in spite of all sad facts and disappointments, keeps saying, "Who knows . . ." With us human beings, hope for a happy future usually rises from poverty and uncertainty; the Christian hope, however, rises from a possession which opens many more vistas for the future. That is why hope is regularly found in connection with faith and love, which are both possessions.[9] But the very fact that we possess makes us feel painfully what we still miss; it "tastes like more." Hope therefore is the fruit of both possession and lack.

We find this quality of hope described in a felicitous way in *The Heidelberg Catechism*, question and answer 58: *"What comfort does the article concerning 'the life everlasting' give you?* That, since I now feel in my heart the beginning of eternal joy, I shall possess after this life, perfect blessedness . . ."[10]

Unfortunately this nature of hope has often been obscured in the course of history, and it sometimes looked as if the Christian hope were only a compensation for what we lack, a "drawing on eternity" which diminished when prosperity increased.[11] So it became an easy prey for Marxist and Freudian interpretations. We will not convince the world that such interpretations are wrong unless the facts prove that the very joy salvation gives us makes us revolt against everything on earth which clashes with it and makes us look forward to the moment in which salvation will triumph over all contradictions.

III

The Language of
the Christian Expectation
of the Future

Christian expectation of the future does not deal with utopias and castles in the air but is based on what faith acknowledges as facts and experiences. This discovery does not end our problems however, for it seems certain that some passages in the New Testament are not in accordance with it. Of course we think first of all of the cryptic book of Revelation with its bizarre images. And next we think of Jesus' words concerning the signs of the end, which we have in three versions: Mark 13, Luke 21, and Matthew 24. But also in this respect we find some difficult passages in Paul's letters to the Thessalonians and in 1 Corinthians 15. Especially the imagery in the New Testament confronts us with difficulties. What are we to do with the cloud, the trumpet, the dragon, the city with the golden streets? It seems as if this imagery leads us again to mere castles in the air and that it belies all that we have said about the method.

That is only seemingly the case, however. We have to take into consideration, of course, that the Jewish world in which the Christian expectation of the future was born was highly interested in the future and that it had developed a special language to express its beliefs. This was not the abstract language of later Western science but the imaginative language of oriental expectation. That language is not ours. It is even only partially the language of the New Testament itself. In comparison with contemporary Jewish literature it is striking how little use even the book of Revelation makes of this so-called apocalyptic language. This implies, however, that the New Testament makes some use of it. Therefore, we have to learn this language, more or less, to be able to translate it for modern man

—if that is possible and desirable. But we shall come back to this point. First we will check whether the use of this strange language is indeed in contradiction to the fact that the Christian expectation of the future should be seen as an extension of experiences in past and present.

We will start with the book of Revelation. No other New Testament book contains more Old Testament quotations than this one. In its pictures and images it resumes the expectation of the Old Covenant but now starting from Christ. Central is chapter 5, in which only the Lamb who is slain—which is at the same time the Lion of the tribe of Judah—is worthy to open the scroll and to start history. And that history wholly bears his mark, for his church also is subject to slaughter but nevertheless finally triumphs with her Lord. The double secret of cross and resurrection continues in history towards the consummation. The Old Testament language is used to express the continuity of this history with the experiences and expectations of the Old Covenant. What seems to be the most bizarre part, chapter 16, about the seven bowls of wrath, appears at a closer look to describe a repetition of the plagues of Egypt, which results in a new exodus of God's people out of oppression by the powers of the world.

As for Jesus' words concerning the signs of the end—the so-called *Synoptic Apocalypse*—all three Synoptic Evangelists placed it immediately before the Passion story. We know that the sequence of the gospel stories is usually not meant as a chronological one, in spite of the frequent use of the word "then." Often related parables and statements concerning one subject are put together. This is also the case here. It strikes us that in all synoptic Gospels statements about the future are summarized right before the Passion story. The themes dealt with are watchfulness, oppression, decrease of love, flight, and finally spectacular natural phenomena and the coming of the Son of Man in glory. It is conspicuous that all these themes recur in the following chapters, which deal with Christ's suffering, death, and resurrection. The disciples cannot keep watch, they flee from the oppression, at the time of the crucifixion there is an eclipse of the sun, and after his resurrection the Son of Man appears to his followers. Of course, these events do not coincide with the predictions of the preceding chapter. But the meaning is obviously that the future will show—on a larger, and eventually worldwide scale —a repetition of what has happened in the crucifixion and resurrection of Jesus.

And now the different images. It is impossible to deal with all of them; therefore, we choose two striking ones, the trumpet and the cloud.

In the great future the last *trumpet* will sound. What does that mean? First we have to consider what the notion "trumpet" meant to the people of those days, who were imbued with the thought world of the Old Testament. Moses was commanded to make two trumpets to call the people to the tent of meeting. Trumpets were also used on the Day of Atonement, at the Renewal of the Covenant, and at feasts in general. The trumpet had a warning sound as well; it summoned to war. We think of the procession around Jericho and of the attack of Gideon. In the book of Revelation new things happen every time an angel blows the trumpet. The trumpet says, "Attention! God starts acting! Be prepared to meet him!" Now it is clear why Christ returns "at the sound of a trumpet of God" and why the great change starts "at the last trumpet's sound." Did Paul think that on that occasion "real" trumpets would be used? I do not think he would have easily understood our question, and if so, he would not have considered it an important one. Of course, it would not be an ordinary trumpet, but the last trumpet, God's trumpet; but what we shall experience when that trumpet sounds will be in a direct line with what Israel experienced when it heard its trumpets.[1]

The notion of the *cloud* plays an important role in the Old Testament too: the clouds of Sinai, the cloud in the desert, the cloud which overshadowed Solomon's temple, the clouds around God's throne, the cloud of thunder in which God appeared to Ezekiel, the clouds of heaven with which according to Daniel 7:13 "one like a son of man" came down to earth. In the New Testament also the cloud plays a special role at the transfiguration and the ascension. Apparently the thunder cloud or the white cloud floating high in the blue sky was for people of those days and regions the expression of the hidden majestic presence of God. Hence the language of the early Christians, who confessed that Christ would come "on the clouds of heaven." Are those "real" clouds? They will be the most real clouds we can think of, the clouds of the history of salvation, of Moses and Solomon, and of the Ascension. Of course they will not be "normal" clouds: they are the clouds of heaven; but they will evoke the feelings which are in a direct line with the feelings of awe which Israel experienced when it saw "normal" clouds.[2]

Rather than analyzing more of these images (the reader can now do that himself), I want to point out how much the way in which they are used confirms our statement that the future is an extension and glorification of experiences which we have already had with God here and now. But at the same time it is necessary to go somewhat deeper into the subject of the language of image in general. The Bible speaks about the future mostly in images. It is a banquet, a feast, a wedding, a city; there will be pearly gates and golden streets, etc. Why all these images? That is a typically Western question. Since the time of the Greeks we have developed the language of the abstract concept and have worked wonders with it. We have raised natural science and technology to unbelievable heights with it. We have mastered nature with it. Therefore, we sometimes think that this is the only language, or at least the only true language. That, however, is a mistake which can impoverish our lives considerably. A child, a mother, a lover, a poet—they all speak a language other than that of abstract concept. When we want not to control nature but to encounter our fellowmen or to praise God, we need a completely different kind of language. We then resort to the language of imagery, the most human language, the language of all ages. And we need this most of all when we want to stammer about the great future, about that which lies beyond the horizon of our experience. Then we speak of stars falling down from heaven—because our whole fixed order will be done with; of golden streets—because that life will be characterized by an exuberance beyond our imagination. In one way we have this biblical language behind us, but in another way it still lies before us. Our conceptional way of thinking clarifies but also impoverishes. When we hear of trumpets, falling stars, and golden streets, we are inclined to take that as exact information from a travel guide. As a consequence we are separated into two groups: the fundamentalists, who say that we have to take everything literally because the Bible says it is so but that the stars might be meteors, for otherwise they could not fall on the earth; and the modernists who say that all this is childish and primitive thinking and that we have left that sort of thinking far behind. Only the poets understand that kind of language because the Bible, when it speaks about the last things, can only speak poetically. Perhaps the best we can do for the time being is to translate those poetical images, to adjust them to our limited hearing and sight if only we will realize then that our translations fall far short of the image. We can pour the future into our concepts, but we run the risk that nobody will long for it anymore. Yet that is all we can do for the present, while waiting for the time in which we shall understand the biblical imagery again straight away, just like poets and children.

IV
Time
and
Eternity

We are not yet finished with the questions about the *methodos*, the access road to appropriate statements about eternal life. The very things we have said about imagery presuppose a certain relation between our life and the future life—a relation which has to be expressed more fully. Questions about *methodos* and content are inseparable. This chapter is designed to show the unity between those two and to lead from the first kind of question to the second. What has been said about the method indicates that between the "now" and the "then" there exists a connection on the one hand and a break on the other. If there were no continuity between the two, we would not be able to talk about the future. And if there were only continuity, this future would be infinitely less than what has been promised to us, and we would not need images to stammer about it. The question of the relation between continuity and discontinuity which comes up here has mostly been treated as the relation between time and eternity. Whether or not this wording is a felicitous one will become clear in what follows. We start from this usage and try to find a way to a solution of this difficult problem with the help of some clear and influential standpoints.

In biblical usage all that deals with the future is often designated by the word "eternal." For that reason one is inclined to characterize our present world as "temporal." Under this aspect the relation between our world and the world to come is primarily seen as a contrast because time and eternity are considered as mutually exclusive realities. Eternity is seen as that form of existence in which there is no before and after, no earlier and later, no beginning nor end—in which past and future are dissolved into an everlasting "now." So eternity is timelessness. Then fulfillment means that time empties itself into, is dissolved into, returns to (or whatever word one prefers to use) eternity. But no matter which word is used, one is always inconsistent because all these words suggest a certain coming after each other of time and eternity and therefore suggest also a certain continuity between the two. But if eternity is timelessness, how can it come after time? And what then is the sense in talking about it in terms of the future? Is there any sense in referring to the future with words like resurrection, second coming, judgment, rejection, and salvation? And can we speak of history as being directed towards the future? Those who talk about the future on the basis of this contrast between time and eternity get into trouble at this point. On the one hand they do not want to abandon the biblical vision of the future, but on the other hand they must challenge it substantially because of their principles. Such wrestling with the problem is found in the earlier writings of Karl Barth, Paul Althaus, Emil Brunner, Reinhold Niebuhr, and others. Althaus says about the Last Day that it will be not an event that comes at the end of history, but one which ends history. This seems a very clarifying distinction at first sight. But on second thought it appears to be little more than a play on words. What are we to think of an event (a word taken from history!) that ends history (and therefore fully belongs to the sequence of moments in time) without belonging itself as ending to that same history?[1]

It is therefore a misunderstanding to think that such a distinction between time and eternity should underlie biblical thinking. This misunderstanding is, however, facilitated by current and even by biblical usage. We human beings do not have words and concepts to express the eternity of God, his being wholly beyond time. The only thing we can say is that God lives very, very long, thus using the largest measure of time we have. This measure is called in Hebrew *olam*, in Greek *aion*. God is called in the Old Testament *me-olam ad-olam*, which means "from way back in the past till far into the future," from eternity to eternity. In the New Testament the word that is used is *aionios*, "everlasting," "eternal." These same words are also used to express what will happen to mankind a long time from now or during a very long time or in a time period that will never end. At the same time they are used to characterize the gifts, situations, and events which are implied in such a never-ending future—for example, "eternal redemption," "eternal home," "everlasting covenant," "eternal inheritance." But we will get quite confused when we do not recognize the discrepancies in this usage. When God is called *aionios*, it means free from time, beyond time. When an *aionios* life for mankind is promised, it means "in a new age," a new time period which will last very long, even endlessly. This difference implies that the biblical terminology embraces two "eternities," that human eternity is something completely different from God's eternity, and that the human eternity is supposed to come about in time.

It is therefore understandable and wholesome that a reaction arose against such an unbiblical distinction between time and eternity. This reaction is especially linked with the name of Oscar Cullmann and his widely read book *Christ and Time*.[2] He rightly points out that in the Bible no distinction is made between eternity and a long period of time. Building on this discovery, he thinks that both God and man partake in the same "temporality," which he represents as an infinitely long line. The difference between God and man lies in the fact that the former partakes in the whole infinitely long line and the latter starts somewhere on the line. That disposes of every qualitative distinction between time and eternity, a distinction which Cullmann thinks stems from philosophical suppositions alien to biblical belief. Eternity, therefore, is nothing else than infinite time.

It is clear where Cullmann's strong point lies. But it is also clear what he has in common with his adversaries. They all start from the principle that similarity in words points to similarity of matter and that when both God and man are called "eternal," this word therefore must be meant both times in the same sense, either as extended time (Cullmann) or as timelessness (his opponents). But this common supposition itself is debatable. Dogmatics should not adjust to the biblical usage but rather point out the essential differences that are hidden beneath it.[3]

So we must maintain against Cullmann that God's eternity as

being absolutely beyond time may not be attributed to man, under penalty of wiping out the limits between the two; but on the other hand we must say with Cullmann that eternity as promised to mankind comes about in time indeed, because we expect it as future, as "the age to come." Time is not something that belongs to sin or that only characterizes our present-day inferior creation, so that it can be thrown away like a useless and inconvenient garment. Time is (together with space) the form of God's good creation; it belongs to the indestructible structures of our humanity. As surely as we will be man in the great future, even so sure is it that we will be this man in time. It is only from this supposition that the strong continuity between this life and the next in the Bible is understandable. It is striking that in all the New Testament passages in which the attention is directed towards the transition of our world to the coming one, this transition is described as a progress in time—a transition in such a way that in spite of the breaks and crises which it brings with it, the border between the two worlds can hardly be drawn; evidently the fulfillment will come about in the same time and space in which our history takes place.[4]

Yet this does not end the matter. There is a certain truth in the wrong idea that man will someday be out of time. For there is not only continuity but also discontinuity. Time goes through an unimaginable crisis and renewal. This does not mean that the future is essentially alien to our present. For also and especially in this our world we experience such discontinuity. We see it in the sequence of the historical, crucified, and glorified Jesus; and personally we get some knowledge of it in our dying and rising with Christ, into which event the Spirit initiates us. The great discontinuity will be the enormously magnified projection of these experiences. Therefore, even the future discontinuity stands in continuity with our present experiences. This implies, however, that we may not think of the coming continuity in leaving aside this discontinuity, no more than we may think of the glorified Christ as an infinitely prolonged historical Jesus of Nazareth. This accounts for such expressions in the New Testament as "For in the resurrection they neither marry nor are given in marriage, but are like angels in heaven"; "flesh and blood cannot inherit the kingdom of God";

"God will destroy both one and the other" (i.e., stomach and food).[5] Expressions are used like "uniformity with the exalted Christ," "a spiritual body," "the vision of God face to face." Such phrases indicate the entirely different character of the great future, in which this earthly existence will be glorified.

That enormous process also affects time. Just as the glorified Christ is the same yesterday, today, and forever and just as the past, present, and future therefore form a new synthesis in him, even so should we think of eschatological time. It will not be a continuation of our time nor a being snatched away from time but a glorification of our temporality. Our time will be glorified together with this earth and our human existence. Of course we do not yet know what we mean when we say that. Properly speaking we can only talk about it in a negative way—a sort of time in which the transitoriness of our existence will be done with, in which there is no discrepancy between the past, the present, and the future. We look to the glorified Christ and know therefore which direction our hope may take.[6]

Our present time and our future eternity are therefore related in a tension of being alike and being different. That is characteristic for the entire relationship between this world and the world to come. From now on we can see even better why the language of the future must be imagery. Due to the continuity meaningful statements are possible, but due to the discontinuity only imaginative language can bridge the distance to any extent.

Finally, to make the transition to the following chapter, we must note that as a result of all that has been said before, we agree, with reservations, with the four subjects that are dealt with in traditional eschatology. We start with the resurrection from the dead, then the second coming, then the judgment, and finally the life everlasting. Our reservation lies in the fact that we consider these four themes not as four successive phases of a great event but rather as four approximations and illustrations of this one event. Sometimes in the New Testament witness the resurrection is central; sometimes the second coming or the judgment or the life everlasting.[7] As soon as we want to link these together as stages, as so often has been attempted, we get caught in strange problems for which there are no answers, or (even worse) we make up artificial answers. In doing so we overstep the limits of our knowledge. We do not deny that we cannot do without a certain element of sequence in time; for example, it is impossible to talk first about the life everlasting and after that about the second coming. The future also, and certainly the transition to that future, is an event, a process. But we, standing on this side of that process, are not able to map it out chronologically. We will therefore speak of the four themes mainly as complementary approximation of one indivisible reality.

V

The Future
as
Resurrection

The Christian expectation of the future is often expressed as expectation of the resurrection of the dead. An outsider who hears this confession may wonder on what grounds Christians make this far-reaching statement about mankind. The answer lies in what has been said in Chapter II about the method of Christian expectation of the future: ". . . in the New Testament the future is the unfolding and completion of that which already exists in Christ and the Spirit and which will be carried through triumphantly in spite of sin, suffering, and death." The word "resurrection" can be a key word to the future, because it is handed to us as such in the encounter with God in past and present.

First of all, this word is handed down to us from the *resurrection of Jesus.* This event may be seen as the center of the whole New Testament. This does not mean, however, that the concept of "resurrection" was completely unknown until that time. This expectation of the future had already emerged in the younger traditions of the Old Testament,[1] and in Jesus' time it was accepted in wide circles, with the exception of the Sadducees. The new thing in the New Testament is that the expectation which was entertained for the future had now become reality in one single person. This fact gave to the faith in a future general resurrection of the dead on the one hand a powerful confirmation and on the other a new substance. The resurrection of Jesus was understood from the future resurrection of the dead and vice versa. From the outset both were inseparable for faith. The present fact had at the same time the meaning of a promise for the future. Because this future-disclosing nature was so immediately linked with the fact itself, Paul could argue, so strongly to our mind, as he does in 1 Corinthians 15:12 f. In that passage in which he addresses people who do believe in the resurrection of Jesus but not in the future resurrection of the dead, he writes: "Now if Christ is preached as raised from the dead, how can some of you say that there is no resurrection of the dead? But if there is no resurrection of the dead, then Christ has not been raised." To Paul the resurrection of Christ means nothing if it is not a promise of a future general resurrection. The risen one is not a solitary one but the first-born. And all through the New Testament this is so. The disciples "were . . . proclaiming in Jesus the resurrection from the dead."[2]

But resurrection is to believers a reality not only in the past and in the future. It exists also in the present as the *working of the spirit of Christ.* There is a close connection between Spirit and life. As it is expressed frequently, the Spirit "makes alive"; the Spirit makes people "born anew" and brings about a "new creation."[3] This working of the Spirit is closely linked with the resurrection of Jesus. Not only is the former based on the latter,[4] but one should even say that the Spirit carries the resurrection of Jesus into our lives, or rather that the Spirit involves us in the resurrection of Jesus. To express this, the New Testament sometimes uses very strong terminology, such as being raised with Christ, and revealing in our existence not only Jesus' death but also his life.[5]

One is almost inclined to think that the resurrection of Christ is fully continued in the resurrection of the faithful here and now. But that is not the case. The term "resurrection," which is always used in connection with Christ, is not used for the working of the Spirit in the believers, and this is not a coincidence.[6] In Jesus' resurrection we are born anew; certainly—but "to a living hope."[7] What is meant by and begun in the resurrection of Christ is not yet fulfilled in what the Spirit works in us here and now. What happens to us makes us eagerly look forward to the future. The Spirit also is no more than the first fruits which make us look forward with eager longing to the complete redemption of our existence.[8] It is therefore a dangerous mistake when some people in their enthusiasm think that the resurrection has taken place already because of what the Spirit works in us.[9] Then one thinks too highly of what he has already and too lightly of what God has promised. Our resurrection here and now is only fragmentary, overwhelmed as it is with our imperfection and sin. Even the Spirit is only a "guarantee." Everything points to a future. But also everything urges us to expect a real future that will mean worldwide resurrection.

The question is whether we can make statements about this *coming resurrection.* Do we only know "that" it will come, or can we also say something about the "what"? The latter is indeed the case if we follow the New Testament. But again it is striking, how much the future is deduced from the past. Not from the present, from the work of the Spirit—that is too much piecework which points back to Christ and forward to the future. But what happened to Jesus in his resurrection enables us to know what is going to happen to those who are seized by the power of his resurrection. For the risen Jesus appeared to his followers. The eyewitnesses stammered about this event in words which reflected their bewilderment and enchantment. They recognized him and they did not recognize him. He was a man among men; he wore the scars of his sufferings; and yet he was strange, for he appeared and disappeared in a mysterious way, and Paul even saw him shining with a marvelous lustre. They saw him, so to speak, while he was on his way from our old world to the glorified world of God. The appearances of the risen Lord took place at the borders of their world of experience and ours as mysterious signposts to the future of God. And since that time they knew that their hopes lay in that direction. What he is able to bring about in us in the great future resurrection is similar to what happened to him in his resurrection. For it is he "who will change our lowly body to be like his glorious body" (Phil. 3:21). In this confession there is no fantasy and speculation about an unknown future. It is simply what is sometimes called an extrapolation, an extension of the lines of experience to a previously unknown field, in this case an explication of the promise given in the fact of the resurrection and change of Jesus. That is why in 1 John 3:2 it is said very soberly, ". . . it does not yet appear what we shall be, but we know that when he appears we shall be like him . . ."

However, in spite of this sober reserve, Christian faith strongly emphasizes that the *body* will be raised. With this confession it is up against the common expectation that an immortal soul, as the indestructible essence of man, will survive death. We believe in the unity of human nature; a body without a soul is a corpse, but a soul without a body is a ghost. Our total human nature will die, even the complex of concepts, imaginations, relationships, and aspirations which we usually call the soul. As counterpart to this conviction, we expect the resurrection of the totality of our human nature. The word "body" in the Bible often stands for much more than what we call a body. We should translate it rather with "person" or "existence," which always includes what we call a body—that instrument which enables us to communicate with the outside world. But the confession of the bodily resurrection is based in the first place not on such arguments but on the fact that the risen and manifested Lord himself had a body. At the same time it is true that "he appeared in another form,"[10] and that will therefore hold true for us too. As Paul says, "It is sown a physical body, it is raised a spiritual body."[11] A spiritual body is not an un-bodily body or a refined body but an existence which also in its bodily aspect has been transformed by the Spirit to be fit for the glorified existence awaiting us beyond the borders of the resurrection.

Linked with this is the question whether the expression in the Apostles' Creed "I believe in the resurrection of the flesh" is a valid one. The English version reads, "I believe in . . . the resurrection of the body." That weakens the expression somewhat but still evokes the same question about the continuity between our present and our future bodily existence. For Paul explicitly says that "flesh and blood cannot inherit the kingdom of God."[12] Our flesh—understood as our perishable and at the same time sinful existence—will, on the contrary, be thrown off in that great future. This also applies to our present bodiliness, which is not something static but a process of building up and of demolishing, with a tendency towards calcification and aging. That body is dissolved after death and taken up again in the great cycle of nature. Resurrection means a radical renovation. But it is not something totally new. "I believe I will rise again—as a completely new person," but also "I will rise again—as the same being." The glory of this expectation lies in the fact that we say both things with equal emphasis. The words concerning the resurrection of the body mean to say that it will be I who will be raised, that this mortal must put on immortality. But we who live at this side of the great renewal cannot know what that "I" will be, which will remain through crisis and renewal. The risen Jesus guarantees our identity; that is enough for us.

Thus from the future a double light is thrown upon our life and our world here and now. God takes this earthly existence with deadly seriousness. Redemption does not mean that this existence will be thrown off like the first stage of a rocket. We do not reach our goal by escaping vertically, nor do we reach it by running on horizontally. This existence will not be ended, nor will it be continued forever. It will be renewed on the analogy of Jesus who was raised from our old existence to a new life. Our life and work lie under the enormous and happy tension of God's renewing yes and no at the same time. This may inspire everyone who strives with courage and perseverance for the renewal of this existence. Then we have no need for further information about that future. It may suffice that we, looking upon the risen Lord, know what Paul means when he says that we shall bear the image of the last Adam, the new man.[13]

VI

The Future
as
Second Coming

The term "second coming" has very different emotional values among us. In circles with a strong and very concrete expectation of the future, this term is favored; one expects Christ's return soon and sometimes even knows when that will be. On the other hand, in the doctine and preaching of the official churches "second coming" plays only a very modest role. Here the term "the coming of the kingdom of God" is preferred. Evidently it is more acceptable to our modern consciousness of life to expect a new order than the return of someone who has lived in the past. The latter conviction sounds to many people more or less mythological.

Yet we cannot deny that many times in the New Testament the future is represented as the personal coming again of Jesus Christ. We think especially of Matthew 24 and 25 with the summons to watchfulness and the parables of the servant who was set over the household, of the wise and foolish maidens, of the talents. All of that deals with a Lord, a bridegroom whom we will meet and whose coming we should anticipate watchfully. Of course we may also speak of the "coming of the kingdom" if only we realize that it includes the coming of the king, or rather vice versa—that the king brings his kingdom along with him. The future is an encounter face to face with God, with Christ, with God in Christ.[1]

Therefore, we cannot find any valid objection to the word "coming," especially not we modern men who prefer to think personally, in terms of "relation" and "encounter." It is a little different when we extend the word to "second coming." That term is not to be found in the New Testament. Of course, this means little since some New Testament expessions like "I come again" mean about the same.[2] But the current expressions are different. The word "parousia," which literally means "presence" (and is generally considered as "second coming") occurs frequently. Another word is "the day," which does not stand for a period of twenty-four hours but is used in the sense in which we say, "My day will come"—to denote an action of decisive importance. The coming of Christ is mostly expressed in forms of the verbs "to come" and "to see." The Son of Man will come according to Daniel 7:13; because of that the believers pray, "Come, Lord Jesus." He will then be seen by his people but also by his adversaries. That moment is also called "appearance." It must strike us that the notion "again" or "second" is missing in all these examples; this coming is not a repetition: it is a unique coming—public, majestic, and active.

Why is so little emphasis placed on the "again"? Because this would suggest that the Lord we are dealing with is at first present and then gone and then present again. This suggestion is not completely wrong; again we think of Matthew 24 and 25, where the Lord is presented as absent for a long time. But yet this does not mean a complete and real absence. That becomes evident when we hear Jesus say, according to Matthew, "For where two or three are gathered in my name, there am I in the midst of them" (Matt. 18:20) and "I am with you always, to the close of the age" (Matt. 28:20). We also think of the book of Revelation, in which the risen Lord is constantly and concretely present as the one who appears to John, who supports the seven churches, and who opens the book of history. The church, which is involved in that history, nevertheless prays, "Come, Lord Jesus!" (Rev. 22:20). It is looking forward to the coming of one who is present already. Should we say then that he is not yet bodily present? No, for his body is constantly spoken of as an earthly reality—the church, in which he, being the head, is present among us.

The most remarkable passage in this respect is found in the last speeches as recorded in John 16:16-22, where Jesus says, "A little while, and you will see me no more; again a little while, and you will see me." To what does that "little while" of not seeing refer? To the time between crucifixion and resurrection? To the time between crucifixion and outpouring of the Spirit? To the time between the ascension and the second coming? We do not know. There is something to be said in favor of each of these views as well as against them. In view of the fact that for John many words have an ambiguous meaning, it seems probable that all three views are meant here at the same time.[3] There is a profound ambiguity in this passage. There is a constant coming and going and coming again It is compared with the pains of childbirth (vs. 21). Every form of leaving which hurts is at the same time a new coming, a further step on the road to the birth of the new man.

Thinking this through, one is almost inclined to see this so-called second coming as the organic fulfillment of the continued coming of the Lord. Yet God's work of salvation is not that organically organized. Here we are warned by the even more frequent image of the final coming of Christ "as a thief in the night."[4] With that it is said that the great future will invade our lives as a totally unexpected intrusion and threat. This image has played and still plays an important role in the expectation of the future of churches and sects. The conclusion is then that the coming in glory will fall into the history of man like a bomb, without any relation whatsoever with what has developed there. But 1 Thessalonians 5, the passage which deals most elaborately with the thief-like character of the future, denies that. It says that those who live without Christ will be surprised by the great crisis, "but you are not in darkness, brethren for that day to surprise you like a thief " (vs. 4). Therefore, Christ says in Revelation 3:3, "If you will not awake, I will come like a thief . . ." For the watchful church this image does not hold good.[5] The question now is what exactly is meant by "to watch"? It is not that we know when that day will come; rather we do not know. Primarily it means reckoning with that future and keeping consciously on our way towards it.

Seeing all this, we find here the same striking ambiguity which we also found when we discussed the resurrection: The future is a break and a turning from our present existence on the one hand but its fulfillment and crown on the other. The New Testament imagery struggles to express those two aspects. The coming of the Son of Man is the last and greatest turn of world history, but he who comes

is already present in the Spirit; his coming is the birth of the new
humanity which the believers see already foreshadowed in the tra-
vails throughout history since Christ's coming in the Holy Spirit.

Now it is time to ask the question, What is the distinctive and
unique character of this last and definite coming? If he who comes
is not absent but rather present, then his last coming cannot be so
much a second coming as a new way of coming and of being
present. First Jesus was present among us in the manner of bodily
human presence as the only representative of a new humanity. Now
he is present among us in the Spirit, through whom he works in a
contagious and renewing movement to conform many people to his
image. And soon the harvest of this process will be gathered—when
he will appear as the center of a world which is re-created in his own
image. Therefore, the new element will be the publicity and the
glory. In our present existence the secret of God-with-us is still
hidden under imperfection and sinfulness. Everyone is still able to
deny—and for good reasons—that in the Christ event which goes
through the world, the decisive and future-disclosing movement is
on its way. But we enter a future in which this ambiguity will be
over; the new man will be revealed such as he was meant by God
from the beginning and in such a way that nobody can deny his
meaning anymore—so that "every eye will see him," including the
eyes of those who have pierced him with their animosity or unbelief
or lukewarmness.[6]

In connection with this we should pay attention to something
that is usually overlooked—i.e., that the one who returns is not seen
in the New Testament as solitary and alone but as the center of a
large human community which forms the kernel of the world which
he brings with him. When he comes out of his hiddenness, the
community which is called his "body" and which came into being
as the fruit of his sacrifice also comes out of its hiddenness and
ambiguity into the light. "When Christ who is our life appears, then
you also will appear with him in glory."[7] This close connection
between him and us makes Paul speak of the church that will be
caught up in the clouds to meet the Lord in the air[8] and makes the
book of Revelation speak about the armies of heaven which follow

him in their white garments.[9] We should let these images be images·
and try to understand their language. They tell us that the issue is
the disclosure of the new man not as a solitary one but as a first fruit,
as center of the "revealing of the sons of God," and of those as the
first fruits of a groaning creation.[10] Then the true church of Christ
will be disclosed as those who have understood the meaning of life
and history and who have partaken in it.

Because Christ has come and is risen, because he appeared again
to work in the Spirit, we trust that the future will be his definite
coming. About the "how" of that event we can only stammer in
images. Perhaps we may finally say it in this way: The time will
come when the countenance of the new man Christ, to whose
likeness the Spirit already now makes man everywhere in the world
conform, will be visible all over this world in a redeemed humanity
of which he will be the source and the center.[11]

VII
The Future
as
Judgment

The third key word to the future, the word "judgment," has for centuries had a dark and forboding connotation so strong that it also influences the meaning of the other key words. For many people this puts the whole expectation of the future in a minor key. This is partly due to what an agelong tradition has made of this article of faith. We may think of the famous medieval song "Oh Day of Wrath" which became a part of the Catholic mass for the dead and which occurs also in many Protestant hymnals.[1]

And who is not familiar, either from a reproduction or from his own observation, with Michelangelo's famous painting of the last judgment on the wall of the Sistine chapel? The central figure is Christ, the irate judge who with a gesture of repudiation turns to the damned who are lying at his feet, their faces twisted with despair. The martyrs who surround Christ encourage him to revenge them. But Mary, seated at the right hand of Christ, turns with horror away from this scene. Is this the way we should visualize the coming judgment?

The Greek words used in the New Testament for "judge," "to judge," and "judgment" (*krites, krinein, krisis*) have about the same meaning as in our usage. They denote a negative action. The judge is the one who condemns. Of course he can also acquit a person, but that is nothing other than not condemning, in which case nothing happens. Should we imagine the coming judgment in this juridical sense? It is striking that the Gospel according to John, which is addressed to Hellenistic circles and uses this kind of language, lets Jesus deny that he should be a judge in this sense: "For God sent the Son into the world, not to condemn the world, but that the world might be saved through him."[2] But elsewhere, also in John, Jesus is explicitly presented as the coming judge. The explanation lies in the fact that the New Testament is written on the border between the Israelitish and the Hellenistic world; it therefore works with a twofold meaning of these words. When Jesus and his disciples use them, the Hebrew usage is involved. The Old Testament words for "judge," "to judge," and "judgment" (*shofet, shafat, mishpat*) are much richer and more positive than their Greek translation suggests. The Hebrew word *shafat* means "to establish the right order of things." In the Old Testament this is particularly the work of God. For the world is out of joint. There are crooked situations here. The just and the meek are trodden down; the haughty and the brutal reign over the world. But the God of Israel cannot tolerate that, as he has proved in the history of his covenant ever since the delivery from Egypt. ". . . it is God who executes judgment, putting down one and lifting up another."[3] He also uses man for this work. In a certain period the men he used were called "judges." In the book of that name we read very little about what we call jurisprudence. The judges appear to be generals who deliver the oppressed people from the hand of their enemies. That is also the king's duty according to Psalm 72, and especially the duty of the great king who will come, the Messiah. ". . . with righteousness he shall judge the poor . . . and with the breath of his lips he shall slay the wicked."[4] That is what God is up to—to establish a right and wholesome order in which the arm of the oppressor will be broken, in which righteousness and love will reign and the meek will inherit the earth.

This work of the divine judge, or the one who makes right, is in the New Testament the work of Jesus Christ. He entered into an established pious order, in which the scribes who explained and maintained the Law came first and in which the people who did not know the Law came last—children, publicans, and prostitutes. In this pious order haughtiness, insincerity, and contempt ruled, and there was no room for the heart of God's work—his free grace for sinners. Jesus came to turn this established order upside down. To the ruling pious persons he spoke his "Woes" and to those who knew that they were condemned by public opinion, he spoke his "Blessed." In several words this purpose of his work comes out very clearly.[5] Especially in Mary's hymn of praise, the very well-known and yet so little understood song, a battle song in the mouth of this humble girl: ". . . he has scattered the proud in the imagination of their hearts, he has put down the mighty from their thrones, and exalted those of low degree; he has filled the hungry with good things, and the rich he has sent empty away."[6] Jesus had come for this revolutionary vindication; therefore, he was crucified. In that he became our savior.

The work of the Spirit is to involve our hearts and lives in this judging, vindicating truth. Only then are we involved in our salvation if we know ourselves as the outcasts, the ones that come last —if we recognize ourselves in the lost sheep and the prodigal son, in the publicans and the sheep without a shepherd. As long as we find our peace in our own status and achievements, we are fatally threatened by God's rearrangement of values and proportions. We are geared to this new order by the work of the Spirit which Paul defines as the justification of the godless. (See Romans 4:5.) That justification is not a passing phase in our life, but the continual starting point of our renewal. To express that, Paul uses the word "to test," "to try" (*dokimazein*). Both the individual and the church must be tested over and over to see whether they still live by grace alone and whether they still really live by grace. Thus we are judged again and again and through the judgment put in the right.[7]

Now we can understand a little better what the confession of the *last judgment* means. God's work of establishing the right order in our lives and in the world is still a long way from being completed. It is still contradictory to the present world, in which impudence and ruthlessness always seem to have the best of it. There is still little to be seen of God's judging, but faith has perceived just enough of it to take courage for the future. On account of what we have seen in the history of Israel and in the work of Christ and the Spirit, we look confidently forward to an eventual liberating judgment which will put straight forever this disrupted human existence. This last judgment will be different from the preambles we can perceive up till now in that it will fully lay bare our present existence—"we must all appear before the judgment seat of Christ"[8]— and also in that it will include "all the nations" so that everywhere the "goats" will be separated on the left and the "sheep" on the right. This well-known passage from Matthew 25 especially impresses us again with the fact that judgment means not only horror but also liberation. Everyone who has put his hope in Christ, in spite of the visible evidence, will in that judgment be put in the right forever. But all the lives that were lived against the grain of God's intention for this world will be inexorably disclosed in that judgment in their lostness.

This leads us automatically to the question of the *criteria* with which we will be judged. The most simple and in itself correct answer is that sincere faith in Christ is decisive—faith like that of the publican in the parable (Luke 18:9-14). But if the publican takes pride in his helplessness, he then becomes another and much more refined Pharisee. It is not for nothing that in the New Testament and especially in Paul the coming judgment is so often spoken of as a judgment through works.[9] This is not a recommendation of legalism, but it says that only a real, a working, a living and effective faith will do in that great judgment. Here, for example, we think of the parable of the rich man and Lazarus; the rich man knew God and his salvation, but he did not want to get actually involved in God's vindicating salvation as far as his neighbor Lazarus was concerned.

On the other hand we may know that faith and works in this life never coincide. It is our consolation that our faith is always ahead of the present reality of our life. It is our shame that our reality always lags behind our faith. For that reason Paul speaks about judgment as he does in 1 Corinthians 3:10-15: It may be that our works are burned up and that we suffer loss, though we will be saved ourselves, "but only as through fire."

Not less important is to keep in mind that this judging involves not only the church but the whole world. Everywhere the groaning creation waits with eager longing for what it expects and hopes for

—"the glorious liberty of the children of God" (Rom. 8:21). The judgment will mean worldwide salvation for the outcasts and the mistreated, for the crushed and the tortured. How could a man with something like a heart left in him keep up with our world if he could not hope for this? In that judgment also those will be put in the right forever, who without knowing of this judging Lord, have become followers of his mercy. In as far as they showed that "what the law requires is written on their hearts," their deeds will be justified in the great judgment.[10]

It is a deplorable fact that the idea of the judgment as hope for the downtrodden has not yet found much acceptance in the Christian church. This is in spite of the major role which the poor and miserable play in the Bible as objects of God's care. For the Old Testament one may read Psalms like 9, 10, 72, 82, 146. For the New Testament we think, for example, of the parables of the great banquet and of the rich man and Lazarus. The poor man is he who cannot help himself and for whom no one stands up. In him the reality of our common situation before God is revealed. Therefore, the poor have the lead when the kingdom is near. Traditional interpretation used to present Lazarus and the other poor ones as the pious poor, which meant mainly pious but by chance poor. But according to the gospel he is truly pious who discovers the reality of his situation before God in his own social helplessness or in the person of his helpless neighbor. For all those the message of the judgment is gospel.

This is how the elder Blumhardt understood judgment. He said that Christ will come to judge—"but note well: not to condemn, but to restore."[11] But we should ask, Is that a contradiction? Judgment is also rejection. But more about this in the next chapter.

VIII
The Future
as
Separation

We have seen that while the last judgment means condemnation, it primarily means liberating and uplifting those defeated by unrighteousness. This does not mean a denial of the judgment as condemnation, the verdict on what the psalmists call "all the workers of iniquity." The judgment which is making straight also means separation. And the confession of the judgment means the confession of the risk we run with our lives.

It would be very strange if we would not pay close attention to this risk aspect of the expectation of the future. Yet it has to be said that it is hardly done in the Christian churches nowadays. This seems unbelievable. But it becomes intelligible when we keep in mind that at stake here is what we usually call "hell"—a subject which embarrasses us. The theological books on eschatology pass it by quickly,[1] and in sermons both the matter and the word are avoided even in those churches which consider the existence of hell as an undeniable doctrinal point. What is the reason for this? There are many jokes about hell, and when somebody mentions the word, he often produces embarrassed laughter from his audience. I hear in that the response to ages of fear for hell. Have we overcome that fear or only repressed it? Anyway, we do not want to hear about hell any longer. We have the feeling that hell has been immensely misused as a threat by people who thus wanted to add weight to their conviction or that the mentioning was a mask behind which resentment and vengefulness were hidden. We think of the church father Tertullian who comforts his persecuted fellow Christians with the thought that in the future they will see their persecutors being burned.[2] We hear an echo of this in article 37 of the Dutch Confession of Faith, saying that the pious will see "the terrible revenge which God will take on the godless, who have tyrannized, persecuted and tortured them in this world." We have become allergic to that sort of language. This makes the whole doctrine about a condemnation and a hell suspect for us. And this feeling has even been deepened by the way in which Christian art (or what passes for that) has pictured this subject for ages—a big fire, goat-footed devils with forks, people screaming in unbearable pain.

That is why we would rather keep away from this subject. For even people who think they believe in hell do not really do so or at least hope they do not have to do so. In this indecision and embarrassment we therefore keep silent. But a wrong way of speaking is not corrected by silence, especially not since there are such clear biblical passages on this subject. Furthermore, we should keep in mind that we do not find those words in the Old Testament, which is often regarded as severe,[3] but in the New Testament and there only very little in Paul but mostly in the mouth of Jesus himself!

To penetrate what the New Testament wants to express on this point, it is necessary to pay attention first of all to the various words and definitions used. What we call "hell" (a Germanic word) is in the New Testament called *gehenna*, a Greek rendering of a Hebrew word which means "valley of Hinnom." The Jews believed since the second century B.C. that in this valley south of Jerusalem, where the horrible child sacrifices had taken place, one day the judgment would come about and the furnace of flame would be opened to devour the godless. Thus this name was also used in the New Testament, in which it occurs twelve times, eleven of which are in words of Jesus in the Gospels.

Yet more often the circumstances of this condemnation are described with words such as fire, everlasting fire, furnace of flames, wrath, eternal wrath, eternal destruction, punishment, outer darkness, weeping and gnashing of teeth. This shows that the New Testament is not interested in determining the place of what we call "hell" (even the word *gehenna* had lost its special connotation in that time), but all the more in indicating the situation in which

condemned men are bound to live. And not less does it emphasize
the connection between that future and the present life. Take a term
like "outer darkness"; it means that a person who chooses to walk
in darkness now will in the great future find himself in the outer
darkness, and that darkness will be very closely related to this
earthly life, for the condemned will look back upon it in helpless
contrition. Exactly that will be his condemnation—that while
weeping and gnashing his teeth, he has to think of what he has
wasted and lost in his earthly life. We also think of the frequently
used imagery of sowing and reaping. Condemnation therefore is the
direct consequence of the decisions made here and now. C. S. Lewis
says in *The Great Divorce* that the condemned are those to whom
God finally says after much patience, "Your will be done."[4]

The New Testament therefore does not support the view that
the condemnation will fall into human existence like a bomb; it is
rather its ripe fruit. And neither does the New Testament support
the view which is alive among many and which is frequently found
in literature that the outer darkness is in fact already experienced
in our present existence in all kinds of loneliness and anxiety. It is
really that our life is lived in a twilight in which nothing is unmis-
takably clear and nothing irrevocably decided. That situation is
reserved for the future. Present and future therefore belong indissolubly together. This shows why the condemnation is not thought
of as something uniform. There is variation and gradation. Every
condemnation is linked with a certain kind of life.[5]

Is it still necessary to note that also in regard to hell, the language of the future is imagery? It has often been pointed out, and
justly so, that "fire" and "outer darkness" are contradictory if taken
literally. It should be unnecessary to make such silly remarks. The
so-called Christian arts have done much wrong in this respect. We
will have to forget a lot of this hell tradition before we will understand again the message implied in these images and expressions.

The point is now to rephrase this message in our own words. But
first we must determine whether that is possible. It might be that
we are dealing here with a conception of faith inherited from the
Jews, which has little to do with the central tendency of the gospel.

This has often been claimed and in itself it is not impossible. But we can only say this if we are absolutely sure of it, for it might be that we only say this because it does not fit in with the gospel as we want to understand it! We should not forget that the gospel has taken up some Jewish ideas of faith and fervently fought others. The fact that the idea of a future condemnation was included (although with considerably less imagery, fantasy, and emphasis[6]) indicates that it belongs in the gospel. How and why, then? Because the possibility of being lost is a direct consequence of the decision-like nature of the gospel. First of all the gospel has the nature of salvation. But it is not true that this salvation overwhelms us and pulls us along in spite of ourselves. Salvation comes to man, and man is a being built to respond of his own free will to God's love by loving in return. We have received the great gift of being able to say yes to him, but with that we also have the mysterious power to say no to him. Salvation does not put aside our decision; rather it occasions it. Christ causes many to fall and many to rise, and the work of the Spirit is "to one a fragrance from death to death, to the other a fragrance from life to life."[7] Salvation brings an enormous risk into our lives.

Often in contemporary theology we find the idea that this risk was removed and taken away since Jesus on the cross has borne for us the horror of condemnation in his being forsaken by God.[8] This is true insofar as this message is believed—but only that far. The message invites to faith, but at the same time it calls forth the possibility of unbelief. Reprobation has been removed by Christ, but at the same time it has come alarmingly near, for "how shall we escape if we neglect such a great salvation?"[9] God fully respects our humanity as being responsible. We ourselves must answer to what we have heard from him, and we ourselves must face the consequences of our response. Hell is the consequence of God's respect for our humanity. And we, who are so proud of our responsibility, must have the courage to think and digest the thought of the eternal consequences of our attitude to life.

This does not mean that we should indulge in imaginations and fantasies. The New Testament does not support this attitude either. We only get to see our "no" to God's purposes projected on the screen of the future. Woe to those who shut their ears to the voice that calls us to the light! For them the future will not be future any more but a fruitless staring back to willfully missed chances, the despair of being accused by their consciences because they did not want to understand the meaning of life. I feel that this is the meaning of the words "where their worm does not die, and the fire is not quenched."[10]

Those, however, who shudder at the thought of condemnation may remind themselves of the fact that these and similar words occur everywhere in the New Testament in the context of invitation and exhortation. Condemnation in the coming judgment—that is exactly what God does not want and from which the preaching of condemnation is intended to save us. But when we take away this dark undertone, we violate the seriousness and respect with which God in his love associates with his human creatures.

IX

The Future
as
Glorification

"I believe in . . . the life everlasting." Thus ends the Apostles' Creed and in a similar way most Christian confessions. That is the last thing to be said, and it is also the goal. It is the most central utterance of the Christian expectation of the future, to which all other utterances are in fact subordinated. It is delightful that we may say this, for it is our deepest desire to live infinitely and happily, and it is great to know that God, who has put this ineradicable desire into his people, guarantees its fulfillment.

But we would not be able to say anything sensible about this tremendous perspective of our life if it were not for the fact that this expectation, like the previous ones, is based on realities which have happened in our own experiences and still happen. In the New Testament it is self-evident that life everlasting not only is future but also exists already. For it has come in Christ in that unique life that he was willing to lose for the sake of God and man and that therefore proved to be real life, which in spite of the loss was carried through triumphantly in the resurrection. He is therefore the resurrection and the life.[1] And this life can reanimate our dead human existence. The Spirit calls us away from that to participation in the life of the resurrection of Jesus. Especially in the writings of John, eternal life is almost completely seen as a life here and now. But also for Paul it holds good that this new reality is already in our midst.[2] That new life is a life in love, in new and renewed relationships with Christ "who is our life" and through him with our brother, as adopted sons and daughters of God our father, and also with our neighbor, our world, our history, and our future. Yet it should be said at the same time that if we are satisfied with this, we have not yet really tasted it. "If for this life only we have hoped in Christ, we are of all men most to be pitied."[3] Why? Because a thirsty man who tastes only one drop of water gets more thirsty than he was before. All God's gifts point towards the future. We know, therefore, that we may think of eternal life as the infinite perspective of what we taste here already in childhood and fellowship, salvation and love, joy and peace. Therefore we can and may stammer about the future eternal life, for we know the direction in which it lies.

The question is now whether out of our broken and limited existence we can say something to the point about this life everlasting. In the heading of this chapter I used the word "glorification." This strange and difficult word was not chosen accidentally. The New Testament often uses words such as "glorification" and "to glorify."[4] To us these terms have become very vague. But to the people in those days who were used to the Old Testament, they sounded exciting, for in the Old Testament, "glory" was used to define an exclusive privilege of God himself. Man had nothing to do with that at all. When Moses prayed, "I pray thee, show me thy glory," God covered him with his hand while his glory passed, so that Moses could only see his back.[5] But in the New Testament the fact is celebrated that the glory of God in Christ has dwelt among us, and through the Spirit of the risen Jesus this even spreads to man. It is said that we see God's glory in a mirror and that we therefore begin to reflect it ourselves, thus being changed from one degree of glory to another.[6] Once it is even said very daringly that we "become partakers of the divine nature."[7] This does not mean that we are deified, but that now we can enter into God's immediate presence without harm. It evidently was the purpose of God from the outset to make man enter into his own sphere, into his glory. We cannot imagine that. For our contact with him who is the source and the purpose of our lives is a contact from a distance; it is never compellingly to be proven, and it is interrupted again and again. But we are bound for the glorification, that is, the participation in a completely renewed and infinitely exalted form of human existence as has been made known to us for a little while in the risen Lord. That gave the direction to our expectation. But it also sets the limits. For then we look in the direction of a dazzling light.

Yet theologians at all times have tried to give some substance to the situation of glorification. That is certainly legitimate when it takes as basis what is already visible and when it is directed not towards information about things we do not know anyway, but towards the strengthening of our joy and desire. The most frequent definition throughout the ages has been the "beatific vision of God" (*visio Dei beatifica*). There are good grounds indeed to describe the great future in this manner. We will then see in an unveiled way God's countenance, which has been shown to us partly in Israel, partly in Christ and the Spirit. In the Bible this desire to see God plays an important role.[8] We can imagine that countless believers throughout the ages considered it the acme of bliss to behold God face to face.

Yet we cannot define our expectation exclusively with this term. It played such an important role in church history because it was especially attractive to the Christians of the first centuries who belonged to the Greco-Roman world. The Greeks are the people of theory, the *theoria*, contemplation. For them to behold the world of ideas and the deity was the summit. When they became Christians, the biblical words about the vision of God appealed particularly to them. This accounts for the emphasis which this idea received in the following centuries. We think for instance of the grand ending of Dante's *Divina Commedia*, when the poet finally ascends to the contemplation and views the Trinity as three circles with a human face in the middle circle; the moment in which his mind understands this, his utmost desire has been fulfilled. In the doctrines of the Roman Catholic Church these trains of thought have been all-important up till now. But also in the Reformation these were well-known thoughts.

The Anglican bishop Kirk, who wrote an important book about the vision of God,[9] rightly points out that it is very wholesome for us active Christians to be freed of ourselves through this contemplation, to be completely oriented to the Great Other One; and that in this stepping outside ourselves, this ecstasy, we come really to ourselves. But we should also keep in mind the limits of this notion. In the vision of God there hardly seems to be place for a relationship to the neighbor and the world. Moreover, it is thought of very individualistically, graspingly, and passively. Nowadays there is not much enthusiasm for this form of desire for eternity. But it is even more important to keep in mind that the idea of the vision of God is too narrow to cover all the essentials of our expectation.

Another key word frequently used to give substance to the idea of glorification is the word "rest." God's people on its way is then compared to Israel in the desert, longing for the promised land of rest. The Epistle to the Hebrews, for example, views the future in this light.[10] The expression of this view has become very well-known through he Mass for the Dead in the Roman Catholic liturgy, which is characterized by the repeated "Give them eternal rest, O Lord" (*requiem aeternam dona eis, Domine*). In the church hymns this also is a leading motive, e.g., in the passionate hymn of Abaelard *O, quanta qualia sunt illa sabbata*:

> O what their joy and their glory must be,
> Those endless Sabbaths the blessed ones see!
> Crown for the valiant, to weary ones rest;
> God shall be all and in all ever blest.

In a form emptied of its meaning we come across this tradition in graveyards: "Rest in peace." But this image, like the previous one, does not mean so much to people in our days as it did to their ancestors, whose life was so much more characterized by heavy work, sickness, and sorrow. We do not hope so much for rest as for new, meaningful tasks. Fortunately the New Testament speaks of that, too. We think of the parable of the pounds where the faithful servants receive new tasks.[11] Rest is not the only thing. This image, too, is onesided. It brings with it the danger of individualism and may suggest boredom, a suggestion which threatens our traditional views of eternity.

In trying to give substance to the idea of glorification, I think of a perfect *community* rather than of a vision of rest. This idea means more to our generation; we do not think individualistically and passively, but for us life consists primarily of relationships in which we actively participate. Then we find the Bible on our side. There the future is seen as a meal, a feast, a wedding, a city, a kingdom. That means in the first place perfect community with the new man Christ in his glorified humanity. But because Christ is the one who unites us with God and our neighbor, the consummation means perfect community with God and our fellowmen. That is what the end of the book of Revelation wants to express when it speaks of eternal life as a city illuminated by the glory of God. In general the imagery of those chapters is very rich and profound. It tells us that even in eternity man and the world will be indissolubly connected, that nature will be completely subservient to culture, that culture will be the fruit of our agelong history of civilization, and that even there the human works of civilization will go on in one way or another.[12]

It should be said again, however, that we look into a dazzling light. If we forget that, we fall back into our small perspectives and start asking questions to which there are no answers. For instance, will we know each other in the life everlasting? Here the counter question of the Dutch theologian Noordmans is appropriate: Do we know each other now? The great future is not an extension of this life; neither is it an eternizing of its joyous or happy or steady moments. The future is not extension but glorification. And this future does not come forth directly from our present lives but only through death. If for Jesus the way to the resurrection went through the cross, then this holds good no less for our unsaved world. Only through a deep transformation do people become suited for a world in which God will be all in all. In that world our deepest desires will come true. But before that we must abandon them and surrender them to him who fulfills them in a perfect community with himself, our neighbors, and the world.

X

The Double Image
of
the Future

One could think that the discussion of the Christian expectation can be ended with what we have said about life everlasting. But then we still have no answer on a difficult question which has interested Christianity for ages. Earlier we called resurrection, second coming, judgment, and life everlasting the four "projections" of the experiences which we have here with God in Christ and the Spirit "on the screen of the future." Now the question of the relationship between those projections forces itself upon us. And this question becomes acute in what we have dealt with in the two preceding chapters: the future as separation and the future as glorification. First we saw the future as the perpetuation of our own responsibility and then as the perpetuation of God's infinite grace. The confession of judgment and possible rejection confronts us, as we said earlier, with the decision aspect of God's dealings with us; the confession of life everlasting as the last and highest reality confronts us with the salvation aspect of God's dealing with us.

The question is now how we should think of the relation between those two. Should we think that God respects our decision against him so consistently that his respect puts an inexorable limit to his will to save all men so that hell will be through all eternity an open wound in the body of the glorified creation? In that case God would finally be powerless. For a believer that is an impossible thought. Therefore, some people say that hell also serves to glorify God and that he has decided before all time to create a multitude of people for the purpose of eternal rejection. When I hear somebody say that, I always hope that he does not know what he is saying. For then we have a God of arbitrariness and cruelty, one who could have taught even Hitler something. Others say, No, but God leaves a lot of people in the rejection which they have chosen themselves. But that does not help either. When he saves us, it is free grace by which he overcomes our "no" to him; why then does he not do that to all men? This way we may have not a powerless God but an arbitrary and therefore again a cruel God, who in his offer to salvation is very noncommittal. Many think that they should believe in exactly such a God. That belief robs the gospel of its power and prevents man from confidence and joy in God.

Should we then think in the opposite direction? That the aspect of decision does not limit the aspect of grace but that on the contrary God's grace puts a limit to our "no"? That there will be rejection but not eternal rejection? But where does that lead us? Do we not then project our wishes on God? If everybody eventually will be saved, why then should we become and remain Christians? Such a doctrine creates careless people.

This discussion in the Christian church is age-old and has often been very emotional. Everybody feels how much he is involved in this question and how much is at stake here. It is helpful, therefore, to examine first of all the New Testament in this respect. It is clear that there are passages dealing with eternal rejection. Revelation 20 knows in any case that the devil and his helpers the beast and the false prophet "will be tormented . . . for ever and ever," and Paul says to the persecutors of the church that they shall "suffer the punishment of eternal destruction."[1] The most explicit at this point is the Gospel according to Matthew, especially in the parables of chapters 24 and 25, although only once are people mentioned explicitly who as those who are cursed have to go into the "eternal fire" or into "eternal punishment."[2] Attempts have been made to mitigate these harsh expressions. Some argue that the punishment is meant to be educative, that the fire is meant to purify, and that "eternal" (*aionios*) should be taken literally in the meaning of "lasting (only) one period (*aion*) Brunner mockingly called this explanation "exegetical chemistry," and rightly so. The words about an eternal rejection may not occur very frequently, but where they occur they are not to be reasoned away. Moreover, such an eternity of reprobation is often suggested in expressions which do not explicitly mention the word.

But there are other ideas also. I will quote only four texts: "For as in Adam all die, so also in Christ shall all be made alive"; "God . . . desires all men to be saved"; "God, who is the Savior of all men, especially those who believe"; "Jesus Christ . . . is the expiation for our sins, and not for ours only but also for the sins of the whole world." Especially in Paul the word "all" plays an important role.[3] It has also been tried through exegetical tricks to let these texts say the opposite of what they clearly say. Augustine gave the still quoted "solution" of understanding "all men" as "all sorts of men"; it has also been said that when God desires them to be saved, this denotes only a wish, not a decision which God will carry through. This also is exegetical patchwork. When we are honest, we have to acknowledge that we cannot smooth out this contradiction in the New Testament.

But now the question of the theological consequences must arise. To answer this question we first have to deepen a little more what has been said before about the method. What we know in faith about the future is not based on some supernatural information or sacred fortune-telling but is, as we saw repeatedly, the magnified projection on the screen of the future of what has already been given to us in Christ and in the Spirit. A second characteristic should be added: This projection does not mean that we sit down and watch it as spectators, either curious or frightened or enchanted. It not only has its origin in the present but also is aimed at that present. The perspectives of the future are meant to be decisive for our attitude towards the present. Under the form of the expectation of the future, God's word is preached to us for the present under the double image it always has: on the one hand promise and consolation, on the other hand warning and summons. The future, therefore, can appear in two sorts of perspectives. For example, to the persecuted church to which the book of Revelation is addressed, it is shown as the heavenly glory with which she is comforted. But in Jesus' parables in Matthew, addressed to a people who were about to reject their Messiah, the future appears as the judgment of the works that are done now. The future is alternately put in the perspectives of salvation and decision.[4]

Do I mean by this that the New Testament statements about the future do not give information? That would be a great mistake. One can only comfort and warn on the basis of facts. But the information is never a purpose in itself. And it is always directed towards specific people and situations. Therefore, all that we read about the future as consolation and warning does not fit together like a jigsaw puzzle. The one who wants to force this, as many well-meaning Christians do, misunderstands the nature of these statements and tries to straitjacket them. The statements of Jesus himself are no exception to this. He knew and proclaimed that the future kingdom had come close in him. In this way he knew of the future as of his own future. But only in this way. Therefore, he can say, "But of that day or that hour no one knows, not even . . . the Son."[5]

With these considerations in mind, we now return to our question: Should the nature of the gospel as salvation give us reason to hope for the eventual salvation of all men, or should the nature of the gospel as decision give us reason to assume an eternal repudiation beside an eternal salvation? We saw that the former expectation is especially supported by what is written in the Epistles, and the latter by the Gospel according to Matthew. I feel that this is not accidental. We pointed out already that the parables in Matthew have a warning tendency and are addressed to Israel, who is about to reject its Messiah and thus lose its calling. Matthew collected these utterances for the Jewish-Christian churches at the end of the first century, who ran the risk of denying the Messiah Jesus because the fulfillment was long in coming and they were oppressed by their hostile Jewish surroundings. Paul and John addressed churches in Asia Minor and Greece, who, in the midst of paganism, have accepted and kept the faith but to whom a continual question and concern must have been what would happen to their unbelieving family and neighbors in the life everlasting.[6] To their comfort they are told that salvation in Christ will finally extend as far as being lost in Adam goes now.

Should we let these statements stand side by side without any link? We rather ought to pronounce them one after the other. In this respect this problem resembles another one connected with it: the relation between election and responsibility. Only he who has recognized his own responsibility and in faith has accepted God's promise may speak about election. In the same manner we should also say that only he who has learned to tremble at the possibility of rejection may speak about the salvation of all men.

God's action in Israel can best illustrate what I mean, because that is the mirror of his action in the whole world. One should pay attention to the way in which Romans 9, 10, and 11 follow one another. The mysterious hardening of Israel is first reduced to God's inscrutable counsel; after that it is attributed to the human disobedience which is punished by God; but finally the punishment is taken away, "For God has consigned all men to disobedience, that he may have mercy upon all."[7] This can only be confessed by the believing church as the last secret. Finally the power of God's "yes" is stranger than the human "no." Otherwise we would be nowhere. This can only be said at the end. But it has to be said at the end if we believe that God is ultimately not powerless or cruel or arbitrary but as we have seen him in Jesus Christ, the one whose mercy for the lost is infinite.[8]

Does this therefore mean that we may hope that the rejection has a limit and that hell means a purification? Yes, we might say that. I know that to many this sounds strange and heretical. But the attitude of these "many" is often strange and cruel; they would immediately warn their nonbelieving neighbor when his house was on fire, but they believe at the same time that he is rejected forever and they seem to be easily reconciled to this fact. Or do they perhaps not really believe it? I think so and I hope so. How could we as a Christian minority live in a de-Christianized world if it were not for the fact that we may believe that God in his mercy knows what to do with all this lack of willingness and power to believe? But at the same time we shudder to think of the deep crisis and purification through which everything has to go first. To be elected to believe already now becomes a matter of both grateful wonder and high calling. James had beautifully summarized these two in the words, "Of his own will he brought us forth by the word of truth that we should be a kind of first fruits of his creatures."[9]

XI

The Future
and
Our Death

Now we also want to see what the Christian expectation of the future looks like under the perspective of our death. It is striking that many Christians through the ages have been interested mainly and sometimes only in this perspective. That interest was sometimes curiosity. What happens to us after death, in the "hereafter"? And sometimes it was frightened concern about the fate of a loved one who died or about their own future fate. Are our dead now in "heaven"? Do they now rejoice before the throne? And will that be our destiny too?

This interest has considerably decreased lately. A generation has grown up more concerned about the future of the world than about its personal spiritual welfare. There are good biblical grounds for such an attitude. In the Old Testament this personal salvation plays hardly any role at all, and the New Testament deals primarily with the expectation of a renewed earth on which righteousness will dwell. But at the same time it should be said that in the New Testament this expectation is closely interwoven with the expectation of a personal participation in this great future. This close connection between the world and the individual has been disrupted for ages at the expense of the world. It did not matter what would happen to the world if only *I* would get to heaven. This connection is now in imminent danger of being disturbed at the expense of the individual.

Neither one of those is permissible, because our human existence stands in a double perspective. On the one hand we are members in the chain of successive generations, and during our lives on earth we contribute to the maintenance, the continuation, and if possible the improvement of our earthly society. On the other hand everybody is the object of God's concern, a personality with a specific secret and destiny. Those two dimensions of our existence cannot be reduced to one or the other. We become unhappy when one is neglected at the cost of the other. But the emphases differ in the different phrases of our lives, in a man or a woman, in east or west. Communism and Buddhism may be considered as two extremes. In the former the individual is sacrificed to the future of the world; in the latter the individual has to find his salvation by withdrawing from the world. In the New Testament, on the contrary, these two belong indissolubly together. That is why we may and must speak about the future not only in the way in which we have done it mainly thus far, in the universal perspective of world history, but also in the individual perspective of our own eschaton, in view of the limit which *my* life reaches in *my* death.

First of all we should ask, What is it "to die" really? But we do not have an answer to that question because we only look at it out of our lives and therefore from the outside. But we do constantly look at it, and we do live with it more or less. Together with life we also experience life's end—death. And this experience is twofold, dependent on our place in this world. On the one hand we seek death as something natural. Everywhere in nature plants and animals die. Without death there would be no room for new life. These two, life and death, keep nature in balance. Thus speaks our intellect. But on the other hand our heart speaks, and it tells us that we are not animals and that the unique secret of our being a person revolts against death. We want to maintain ourselves in life and we fight death to our last gasp. Thus we are swinging between acceptance of death and terror of death.

As Christians we know of something else besides these two extremes, namely of death as an object not only of acceptance or terror but of expectation. We owe this knowledge not to any special information and speculation about the "hereafter," but to the unique life and death of Jesus in which we are involved. Jesus has lived in our midst as the new and true man. He did not accept death with resignation, but neither did he rebel against it to save his life.

He experienced his death as the test for his life. His life was truly unique. It was not self-maintenance but a continuous giving of himself to God and men in order to make room for the Other and the others. When he finally paid the last price, he was as John says, "glorified." Exactly this radical giving up was the summit of the development of this unique life of love. For in complete giving up is complete life. We with our self-maintenance and our fight against death do not believe that. Jesus believed it with his whole existence. If a grain of wheat dies, it bears much fruit; only he who wants to lose his life will keep it. Therefore, God has exalted him through death and bestowed on him the name which is above every name.[1] For this death was neither a natural fate nor the defeat of a self-preserving existence but the fruit of a new life and therefore the transit to a new life.

Ever since then, people are incorporated in that death through the Holy Spirit. In their baptism and faith they are crucified and raised with Christ. This becomes already somewhat perceptible in their lives now. Paul uses difficult words for this reality. They kill their own sinful bodies; they kill the deeds of their self-preserving bodies through the Spirit. He himself carries the death of Jesus in his body and is always being given up to death for Jesus' sake—yes, he wants to become like Christ in his death in order to share his glorification.[2] This means that for the believer life and death, if seen under the aspect of Jesus who died for us and was raised, look differently. Life in the self-denial of love becomes death, and so it becomes a new life which in conformity with the life of Christ will develop through the last dying into true life. But it has to go through this dying, because our present life is a provisional and sinful existence. We live with death before us to make us realize that even the best we give at this side of life is only a trifle; we have to be dissolved in order to give ample space to the powers of the Spirit in our existence.

When we ask what it will be like, we come out again with the confession of the resurrection of the dead. Here we see how according to God's purpose the universal and the individual aspect, the kingdom and the fulfillment of the individual, coincide. In one breath we may say that we expect a renewed earth on which righteousness will dwell and that we expect to be present there ourselves in whatever way that may be. It is one and the same future that beckons to us in the fulfillment of history and through the gates of death.

And yet it still holds good that these two aspects of this one future do not entirely coincide. This accounts for the fact that when dealing with the future along this very personal line, the line of death, questions arise which do not come up when the future is dealt with under the other perspective. This holds particularly true for the often asked question, How should we visualize the fate of the individual in the time between his death and the universal resurrection? In the New Testament, where faith in the nearness of the kingdom prevails, this question comes up only casually. But we can imagine very well that the few texts on this subject became very, even abnormally, important in later-day faith and theology.

The New Testament often seems to say that our dead are a-sleep.[3] Some theologians build on this expression by saying that the dead are radically "beyond time"; they fall asleep when they die and they wake up at the last day, and to them there was nothing in between. Saying so makes an unbiblically strong contrast between time and eternity (being human is in itself always "being in time") and clearly contradicts other statements in the New Testament. The exact opposite is the traditional view which is found everywhere in Christian churches: that the faithful immediately after their death are admitted to the vision of God and the rejoicing before the throne. Because of the problem that the last day has not yet come to pass, this traditional conception sees only the souls ascending to God's throne, with the bodies being added in the resurrection. Especially the visions of heaven in Revelation have inspired this idea, and also the words in the Epistle to the Hebrews about "the heavenly Jerusalem" with its "festal gathering" and "assembly of the first-born."[4] In our time much protest has been uttered against this view. In the New Testament man is seen essentially as a unity, not divided—here the soul and there the body. In the New Testament the word "soul" means either the total man or the kernel of our existence, the "I." The division between soul and body is not biblical but an age-old inheritance of the Greek philosophy of substance. In that philosophy the concept of the immortal soul is found, while Paul says it differently—namely, that this mortal must put on immortality in the resurrection.[5] This corresponds to the fact that the New Testament writers almost always jump with their thoughts from the present to the great resurrection because only then does everything really begin. He who denies these accents and directs his attention only to an intermediate stage after death ignores and misses the great expectation of the future.

It was no wonder that a reaction arose that did not want to hear of an intermediate stage any longer. According to this view man dies completely to be raised completely at the last day. This concept, however, does not do justice to the continuity between this life and the life to come nor to the conviction in the New Testament that nowhere, not even in death, will we fall out of the hands of our Lord.

Finally we must mention the Roman Catholic view that this intermediate stage is a purgatory, a time of purification, a steady procession towards the light. This view is not to be rejected so easily as it often is in Protestant circles. The opposite view, that the believer after death has lost all his sins and defects as if by magic, has many objections also. The Holy Spirit involves us here on earth in a process of growth. Why should this be cut off so abruptly after death? But we cannot do more than ask questions at this point. We find hardly any grounds for an answer based on the Bible.[6]

The New Testament does not give fitting answers to the questions asked here. They are mostly ignored. Sometimes they are vaguely answered in terms of sleeping or of singing and feasting and in one place by the image of the dead who cry out from under the altar for the justice of the coming world.[7] Time and again being with Christ is mentioned as the essence of our personal expectation.[8] That is simple, clear, and sufficient. Across the border of death our "I"—whatever that may be—remains on its way with him who is our life until the light of the great future dawns. Calvin expresses this carefully and beautifully: ". . . the souls of the pious . . . enter into blessed rest, where in glad expectation they await the enjoyment of promised glory, and so all things are held in suspense until Christ the Redeemer appear."[9] This means we expect to be happy while waiting for the great happiness. The strongest and simplest confession is found on the tombstone of William the Silent in Delft: "He awaits the resurrection"—*expectat resurrectionem.*

XII

Eschatology
and
Futurology

It is not necessary, I suppose, to argue the importance and urgency of this theme. Nevertheless, so far as I know, in theology we have so far taken hardly any steps in this field. That is understandable, however, for several reasons. The talk about futurology came over us only in the last years in a sudden, swelling wave. At any rate in my country it is now the fashion to mention the year 2000 in sermons and addresses. But what is the content of this slogan? Futurology is such a very young science that no one knows what the results are which people can use in other sciences and in practice. And can we call it a science at all? If so, we must call it the science of guessing. Not only our intellect but also our will is involved in projecting the future. Also a creative imagination is needed to work in this field. In what direction do we want to steer the development? The main thing, however, is that futurology borders upon anthropology and is dependent on it. But man is the most enigmatic animal we know. Can we ever predict his attitude? Can we predict more than that it will be always unpredictable? And what if that unpredictable animal with his strong aggressiveness and his weak morality will make another war, this time a nuclear world war? For all these reasons it seems entirely justified when a reality as dignified as systematic theology does not want to have anything to do with this kind of popular fantasy!

There is, however, another side to the question. Man may be unpredictable, but all individuals have a certain human nature in common. We know something about the common ideas and ideals, desires and fears, which determine the behavior of millions on this planet. There is the desire for prosperity and the fear of war. There is the struggle for higher and longer life, for more health, more wealth, more comfort, more leisure, more liberty and equality. Given these inclinations, there is a lot to predict with a certain likelihood, of course always on the condition of lasting peace. The method which futurology follows is that of extrapolation. It prolongates existent developments into the unknown field of the future, supposing that man will have the same concerns in the next half century which he shows now.

This method of prediction by extrapolation is not watertight. A colleague at my university of Leiden, a specialist in the history of art, conducted research in the predictions made around 1900 about the fashion of women's clothing in the coming half century; the result was that these predictions completely failed because they were far too much bound to the range of fantasy and fashion of their own time, and so they underestimated the changeableness of man in general and women in particular. Using the method of extrapolation (and we have none other), we are still in danger of merely reflecting our own situations and limitations. However, we must make a distinction here. There are fields in which man's imagination and changeableness have much room for operation. It would be unwise and impossible to predict the situation of arts, literature, religion, and morals in the year 2000. But in other fields the development is far more bound to the achievements of today, so that we can survey more or less the latitude of progress for the next thirty or forty years. That is the case in science, in technology, and (to a lesser degree) in the behavioral sciences. We can predict something of the progress in medical science, of the manipulation of the genetic code, of the wide role which computers will play, etc. If futurology limits itself to these fields, as it does more and more, it can afford a substantial contribution to preparing man for the decisions which he will have to make in the coming period.

But now, what does theology have to do with the brave new world which futurology depicts for us? We can understand that Christian ethics will have a lot to do with it. But what for heaven's sake is the interest of dogmatic theology? The answer is that this interest is exactly for heaven's sake, which at the same time is the sake of the earth. There is a striking formal parallel between the expectation of the Christian faith and the anticipations of the near future which thrill man in our time. Both direct our attention towards the future. Our faith is in all its aspects a future-directed faith, from Abraham to the Apocalypse. All God's revelations in history are signposts toward his great future. With Barth we may say, "If Christianity be not altogether thoroughgoing eschatology, there remains in it no relationship whatever with Christ."[1]

This is only a formal parallel, however. The content of the expectation seems to be widely different. Eschatology teaches us to believe in the resurrection of the dead, the kingdom of Christ, a new heaven and a new earth in which righteousness will dwell. Preceding this new age there will be, according to eschatology, "signs of the time" or "signs of the future" such as the worldwide proclamation of the gospel, a great apostasy, persecution of the faithful, the coming of the Antichrist, and according to some also the conversion of Israel and a Millennium. These latter two points are controversial, so that the common belief about the signs of the time is preponderantly dark and negative. The common Christian expectation accordingly is that mankind will grow worse and worse, that we have to expect a steady and accelerating deterioration of the world and the church, from which only a sudden intervention of Christ will save the faithful.

The expectation which futurology offers (under the condition of peace) is very different, almost directly opposite to this. Its picture is very bright and optimistic. In the year 2000 automation will control large fields of our civilization. Many decisions which now have to be made as the fruit of mature consideration will then be made quickly by computers. Prosperity will increase more and more. As a result the time for necessary work will be less than one's free time. Infirmities of old age will be reduced to a minimum, and the duration of life will be raised to 100-125 years. The climate will be improved, deserts irrigated, seas drained. There are even plans to divert the warm Gulf Stream—maybe palms will grow in Helsinki! In no time people will be transported to recreation areas elsewhere on this planet. The quality of posterity will be raised by influencing the genetic code. Psychopharmacology will regulate the human moods and in general, if necessary, manipulate people in such a way that they will behave correctly in society. This may now seem to many a gruesome fairy tale. But would our great-grandparents have thought differently of the world in which we live today? Countless research persons everywhere in the industrialized world —biochemists, technicians, physicians, sociologists, etc.—are enthusiastically devoted to the preparation of this near future, in which the problems of life and society seem to find their solution.

What does this future of science have to do with the future of faith? They belong to two different, if not opposite, worlds. And the world of futurology is to many of us far more near, concrete, and attractive than the world of eschatology. But in the world of futurology God is no longer relevant. There is nothing beyond man as subject, and nature and man as objects of a great process of manipulation. Man is the absolute master in his world. God seems to belong to a time when man felt more dependent on the powers of nature in which he could believe to experience the superior power of God. But since man approaches now the culmination of his dominion over nature, God does not meet him any longer and he does not need God anymore. Futurology is atheistic. In this climate the proclamation of an end of our age and the rising of a new earth by divine intervention must sound like mere mythology. And if a Christian, who at the same time really lives as a modern man, believes in both the futuristic and the eschatological future, he cannot find the way from the one expectation to the other and is fated to live in a kind of schizophrenia.

However, this negative conclusion is just as overhasty as the positive one was. There are many aspects of the question to be taken into account before we can arrive at a conclusion. First we must direct our attention to some important similarities between eschatology and futurology. We noticed that futurology rests upon the method of extrapolation. Here we must say that the same holds good of biblical eschatology. It does not deal with supernatural information or wishful thinking, but its statements are founded on what we in faith have experienced about God in Jesus Christ and in the Holy Spirit. If we believe in the resurrection of the dead, it is because we know about the resurrection of Christ as the first-born. If we believe in a kingdom of peace and love, it is because we experience already now the love of God poured into our hearts through the Holy Spirit. This is clearly indicated in Scripture. "If the Spirit of him who raised Jesus from the dead dwells in you, he who raised Christ Jesus from the dead will give life to your mortal bodies also through his Spirit which dwells in you" (Rom. 8:11). "Now if Christ is preached as raised from the dead, how can some of you say that there is no resurrection of the dead? But in fact Christ has been raised from the dead, the first fruits of those who have fallen asleep" (1 Cor. 15:12, 20). "Blessed be the God and Father of our Lord Jesus Christ! By his great mercy we have been born anew to a living hope through the resurrection of Jesus Christ from the dead" (1 Peter 1:3). ". . . it does not yet appear what we shall be, but we know that when he appears we shall be like him" (1 John 3:2). ". . . hope does not disappoint us, because God's love has been poured out into our hearts through the Holy Spirit which has been given to us" (Rom. 5:5). This kind of quotation can be multiplied. New Testament eschatology is the extrapolated projection on the screen of the future of our Christian experience here and now. Because we know that this experience comes from God, that he acts in our sinful world with grace and love and peace, it is implied in this very knowledge that he will not rest until this movement of his love has prevailed over all that contradicts it, all sin and suffering and death—that he will not rest until this whole world is re-created in the style of what he has begun in Christ and in the Spirit. Futurology and eschatology both extrapolate present experience. Their projections differ according to the difference in experience. What is central in the one experience is marginal or nonexistent in the other. But the approach to the future, the *methodos*, is the same. And as a consequence there is a similarity in the sense of life created by expectation and therefore in the structure of belief; for both attitudes the future has priority over the past and the present. For both it is true that the future has already begun. Both can say with Nietzsche, "What shall be and must be is the ground of that which is."[2] No wonder that a group of younger theologians like Ulrich Hedinger, Gerhard Sauter, and above all

Jürgen Moltmann feel congeniality with the Jewish Marxist thinker Ernst Bloch and his great work *The Principle Hope*. As in a former decade the left wing of Protestant theology found existentialism congenial, so now the younger generation of the right wing is open to the wave of futurism which comes over our civilization.

This congeniality is not limited to method and structure but affects also the content. What futurism plans and what eschatology expects is a new earth in which righteousness dwells—a culmination of the dominion of nature, in which man shall reign forever; in which the trees yield their fruit each month; in which the sea will be no more and the dark powers of chaos will be transparent, bright as crystal; and where nature is dominated not by an agressive and divided mankind but by fully developed human powers so that there will be welfare and prosperity for all, the downtrodden will be uplifted, the hungry filled with good things, the sick healed, and the eyes of the blind opened—in short, a kingdom of liberty, equality, and fraternity.

It is a great thing to be able to speak about this convergence in perspective between eschatology and futurology. In the plans and hopes of the futurologists we hear the groaning of creation, longing to be set free from its bondage to decay and to obtain the glorious liberty of the children of God. And everyone who now struggles for a better, a more humanized, world may know that God with his planning stands behind him and goes ahead of him and speaks his effective yes to all the attempts of our time to defeat tyranny, discrimination, disease, poverty, suffering, oppression, and war. All these powers are our enemies and his. We try to expel them and he will finally and definitely do so in his great victory.

Now, however, we must turn the page—not to repeat what we have said in an earlier stage, but to go a step further and to look deeper into the theme. Then we will inevitably discover that this congeniality and agreement is not the deepest level of the question. There are even more levels below. We discover the next one when in this context of agreement we turn anew to the question of divergence between eschatology and futurology. We think of the widely read book of Harvey Cox, *The Secular City*, in which he brings the kingdom of God and the modern city as near to each other as possible. In the mobility and the anonymity of life in the great society he discovers the way of life of the kingdom of God. All failures and faults in the secular city are there in spite of its structure and are a survival of the bad town structures in which mankind had to live in former ages. As soon as we see the kingdom of God and the result of man's planning brought so close together as Cox does, we must suddenly keenly feel the deep and lasting difference between the two ways of expectation. If we as Christians would orient ourselves mainly upon a futuristic concept, we would be in danger of making the ultimate goal of humanity something less demanding than God himself does. What he promised goes beyond our futuristic planning and capacities.

To make that clear, we must start with the nontheistic character of futurology. It is interested only in man's dominion over nature and in his social behavior and rules. Religion is a free-time activity without involvement. One's relation to God plays no role in the shaping of the future. In eschatology, on the contrary, this relation is decisive. In the great future it is God who will be all in all. According to our Christian conviction futurology works with a distorted and defective concept of man. Without the right relation of sonship, surrender, and obedience to God, we cannot expect a truly and permanently humanized world. Love to God and to our neighbor are opposite sides of the same coin. Mankind has to go through new experiences in order to discover that our relation to our neighbor and to nature is indissolubly connected with our relation to our creator and redeemer.

That brings us to a second point. Futurology is interested in the control of nature and in social behavior and structures. It can renew many aspects of human life, but it cannot renew man himself. So the main guarantee for a stable, happy future is lacking. Many futurologists are aware of that fact. They see clearly that we do not gain real ground unless ethical renewal keeps pace with technical and social development.

However, the situation is worse than that. It is not that man remains unchanged within the context of the year 2000. That is impossible. Man changes his social context, but it is also the other

way round—social context changes man. In what direction will
man be changed? Because of the large amount of free time and the
many possibilities open to him, man will be thrown back upon
himself to an extent never seen before. Until now almost every man
has been mainly occupied with the struggle for life and with working at his job. Mankind as a whole is mainly occupied with the fight
to subjugate and control the powers of society and to resist all the
social, economic, and political threats which meet us. What will
happen if these elements are eliminated? This is more than a question about the unknown. There are now already some highly developed nations and areas which show a glimpse of the coming world
society, for example, Sweden and California. Such societies show
high rates of suicide, alcoholism, and use of psychedelic drugs. And
also increasing are phenomena of aggressiveness and sadism (mur-
der, cruelty, etc.). How is that possible in such a happy society?
Because now that man is thrown back upon himself, he can use
most of his energy for his own interests. Some, and we hope many,
will develop a creativity which until now had no chance for development. But some others, and I am afraid they will be more numer-
ous, will see the way open to their aggressiveness, which until now
was partly suppressed and partly sublimated in their daily work.
And some others, and I am sure many, will fall into what is now
called boredom. They do not know what to do with themselves.
They have all kinds of opportunities for relaxation, amusement,
eating and drinking, traveling, etc.; but as soon as they have experienced these opportunities to a certain degree, they get "fed up"
with them all, and because they have nothing within themselves to
give substance and meaning to their lives, they look desperately for
new thrills and adventures. Our capital Amsterdam has the dubious
fame of having given birth to a new species of man, the provo:
artists with beards, nonconformists who provoke and resist the
police in a nonviolent way. America created the hippies, and parallel phenomena are increasing all over the world. The revolting
students in the developed countries are partly to be understood
against the same background. What they have in common is a life
without challenges, risks, and adventures—a life from which they
want to escape either by creating a new, risky world or by living

against the grain and laws of our existing world as in Zen Buddhism or by dreaming away into a mystical supernatural world by using psychedelic drugs.

These phenomena are a foreshadowing of what will happen when man will have attained a culmination of prosperity and liberty. This new world will not renew him but will reveal man as never before in his ambivalence and ambiguity. We may expect new expressions of his creativity but also new outbursts of his aggressiveness, of his boredom, and of his will to escape. Man's problems will not be solved but will manifest themselves in a much magnified form. Our poets, novelists, dramatists, and scriptwriters already sense with a shudder this coming age. Our engineers, biochemists, and sociologists to the contrary prepare with eager longing for this perfectly manipulated world. They trust that they will solve even the problems of human behavior. Why should we not try such means as drugs to oppress the feelings of boredom and revolt and to keep man quiet? But would we then still be ourselves, still be men? Would that not be the most horrible estrangement from ourselves? Would not man himself then be the price to be paid for entrance to this brave new world? But on the other side, what is the alternative? When we remove all threats from nature and society, will we not discover then that man becomes a threat to himself?

Now the question is what all this means for our subject. It reminds us of the fact that the future of unrenewed man and the future of God by their very nature cannot be identical. The promised eschaton is a deed of God which lies beyond all projects of our futurology. It seems that we here come back to the famous discussion in the Stockholm Conference (1925), where the Americans (roughly speaking) expected the kingdom of God as the result of human endeavor, whereas the Europeans expected it as a divine intervention apart from human developments. Is this what makes the difference between futurology and eschatology? So Jürgen Moltmann put the question in some of his articles following his well-known book *Theology of Hope*. He there makes a distinction between *futurum* and *parousia*; *futurum* is related to the Greek *phuo*; it is that which grows; *parousia* is that which comes from the other side. I am not so happy with this distinction. God's future is not unrelated to our history and its developments. It will not be thrown into our existence like a bomb. As we have said already, the future will be the projection and extrapolation of developments which have taken place in our history. The main anticipation of it is the resurrection of Christ and in conjunction with it, the outpouring of the Spirit, which aims at the renewal of man. So God's future will be in some way the result of concrete historical events and movements in which man is not only involved as a passive object but also re-created into an active subject, a cooperator with and under God. In it there is an element of *phuo*, of growing, as is frequently stressed in the New Testament in the parables and images about grain, sowing, ripening, and reaping. But it is true that this movement of God stands at the same time in discontinuity with our natural developments. The incarnation of a new man, of *the* New Man Jesus Christ, is discontinuous with our history, and his resurrection even more so. Therefore, it is the case that God's eschatology is the outcome of a divine process of renewal, which will be completed and crowned in his great future, whereas futurology deals with the human process of development within the scientific, technical, and social sphere. Both are rooted in our history but in entirely different histories which take place on quite different levels.

This can be underlined when we think of the fact that not only the resurrection but the cross and the resurrection together form the great discontinuous center of the life of Christ. The crucifixion of Christ is first of all a human deed in which we reveal once for all what our deepest relation toward God is. As soon as God comes to meet us with his renewal, we resist him at all costs. We feel threatened by this renewal and therefore we have killed the author of life. As far as we are concerned, God is dead and as Nietzsche has rightly added (what the God-is-dead theologians have obscured) "we have killed Him"! That is what man is like—refusing to be renewed, trying at all costs to continue and to embellish his unrenewed life. But the cross is also a deed of *God*. He turns our natural life into death in order that it may be renewed according to his purpose. And we are invited to be renewed according to the image of the crucified and risen Christ and in the power of his grace to take up our cross and follow him in dying and rising, becoming like him in his death, that we may attain also the resurrection from the dead.

When we consider the central meaning of the cross as the medium between the earthly life of Jesus and his exalted existence, we see that the cross is the very link between what we call "ordinary human life" and the life of renewed humanity. That is the way in which the old and the new age are related to one another. Renewal comes not as a result of organic growth nor as a bomb, but through the crisis of dying and rising. That means continuity and discontinuity in one. Therefore, the New Testament can speak of the eschaton on the one hand as the crown of an evolution—as a fruit, a harvest, etc.—and on the other hand as an interruption, an intervention, a thief in the night, an earthquake, a cosmic fire. The eschaton is both or it is neither. It is a crisis or, to put it in the words of Romans 8, it is the result of a travail, a new birth. About that crisis the different New Testament traditions speak in different ways. But all see that the two lines revealed in cross and resurrection, the line of man's rebellion and the line of God's superior power, will both continue and be deepened and strengthened until they both reach a culmination point and a crisis. That is what the images about the antichrists and the Antichrist and about the Millennium and the great last struggle seek to express.

All this underlines, as I said, the difference between eschatology and futurology. But not only the difference, as we now see. God's future has to do with this our present life, its futurological prospects included. He leads it toward a crisis and through that crisis toward his renewal. As a consequence of it, we can no longer say what we said before, that we can separate eschatology and futurology as two levels. God's future lies in the perspective of our future. Our future is involved in that history which he, according to his work in cross and resurrection, leads towards his future. That is a question of faith. We believe this even if we cannot indicate how our present and near future are related to God's eschatological plan. But sometimes it may be possible that we more or less dimly believe we can discern this relation in the concrete events of history. The human future which we expect has on the one hand millenarian and on the other hand antichristian perspectives. We expect prosperity and creativity and also boredom and aggressiveness. We expect that these opposite tendencies which were always present in a more or less hidden way will be revealed in coming times in such intensity as never before. They can create utopia or doomsday. Much depends on the happy or horrible few who will have the control over the political and nuclear power. It makes all the difference whether their name is John Kennedy or Adolf Hitler. The human world will become more ambivalent than ever before. Will that mean that the human future which we expect and plan for will be the instrument of God's eschatological crisis? That could be. We cannot say more. We are no prophets. We deal here with, so to speak, thought experiments. But such experiments are necessary, lest we lose the relation between our faith and our ordinary life. Such thought experiments may be right or wrong, but they remind us of the fact that our planned world and God's promised world belong to one and the same created reality. And so they encourage us as Christians not to feel bewildered and confused when we hear about the perspectives of the year 2000 but to believe that they are part of God's great history and future.

What does all this mean for the attitude of Christians and the Christian church in this age of futuristic planning? Our first and basic attitude will be a positive one. It is meaningful to enter into this world of expectations and manipulations. Whatever the outcome may be, it is taken into the great and all-embracing plan of God. Our future will be a phase on the way towards God's future. The future which we are now creating is a very risky and even explosive one. But even if all this would lead to the greatest crisis the human race has ever seen, this crisis will be part of the travail of the eschaton.

There is also a more specific reason for a positive attitude. The conscious purpose of our future-planners is in general a good one. They want to realize a far greater extent of humanization of our world than we have at this point. They want to outlaw war, oppression, disease, poverty, and discrimination. They want what God also wants and what he will bring in his kingdom. These endeavors and their results may be seen as "signs" of the kingdom. No Christian can be in doubt where his position has to be in these endeavors. He has to be found on every front where dehumanization is opposed and humanization is promoted. And we must acknowledge that this is the very ethical driving force behind futurology.

When we now speak in terms of ethics and ethical decisions, it is also self-evident that Christians, probably but not necessarily more than others, will be aware of the great risks and threats of the brave new world which we are preparing. They share the ethos of the futurologists. They do not share the faith in the positive powers of man which underlies this ethos in the heart of so many futurologists. Therefore, they will be keenly alert to the shadowy side of this new world. They will have to begin now to study the problems of free time, recreation, boredom, psychedelic drugs, etc., and to ask what measures or initiatives in the realm of instruction, pastoral care, education, and politics the Christian church can take to help prevent the dark forces of dehumanization from swallowing up those of humanization, to help the signs of the kingdom prevail over the signs of the antichrist.

As Christians we will have to fight this good fight (I hope together with many other people of goodwill) on the firm rock of a deep trust in God's guidance over this turbulent and ambiguous history. His power far transcends our efforts. He will win in the end. We are his co-workers. But all we can do is to prepare the way of the Lord. He will win, partly through our victories and achievements, because the glory and the honor of the nations will be brought into the heavenly Jerusalem. Our efforts will not be in vain. God will use them. But in his inscrutable sovereign power he will use our failures and defeats as well. That does not take away our responsibility. But it can take away our overstrain and despair.

This cannot be our last word, however. For God's future, though using our future as its instrument, lies beyond our efforts. It means far more than development. It means renewal. It means far more than extrapolation. It means conversion. The New Testament has two words for "new": *neos* and *kainos*. Sometimes these words are used as parallels. But mostly they are used differently. In this case *neos* means something that did not exist before, that arose just now. It is something for a moment or a year or one period. After that it becomes old or obsolete or antiquated. *Kainos* is the fruit of an inner renewal, of a regeneration. The opposition between the old and the new man is a question not of chronology but of way of existence, not a horizontal but a vertical event.

Now both dimensions are in God's hand, and they will be reconciled in his future. But in our sinful world they often lie apart. That makes the attitude of the church so complicated. She will support all endeavors to make new those things and situations which until now were bad. She will take the side of progress. But she has also to fight another fight—for the renewal through Christ and the Spirit. That is her lonesome battle. Here she has no partisans. The world appreciates us when we fight for the new. The world is hardly interested in our fight for the renewal in Christ. But that is our main calling. Development belongs to God's work in history, but renewal is the ultimate aim which even development has to serve. We need wise and humane architects of the human future. We must challenge the most capable of our younger Christian generation to devote their professional lives to that grand task. But the first task of the Christian church in respect to that future will be to create men who live in the mainstream of renewal, flowing from the cross and the resurrection towards its great extrapolation in the crisis and the kingdom of the future. God calls renewed men to serve their neighbors for Christ's sake. On the fertile soil of the promise in Revelation 21, "Behold I make all things new (*kainos*)," we are called to work steadily to make God's world new (*neos*).

XIII
Trends in Twentieth Century Eschatology

At a point not later than the 1799 publication of Schleiermacher's *On Religion: Addresses in Response to its Cultured Critics*, Terrence N. Tice, translator (Richmond: John Knox Press, 1969), systematic theology entered a basically new phase, the consequences of which are not yet entirely surveyable. From then on in theology it was no longer the many-sided display of Christian truth and the polemics against heresy which was central, but the interpretation of the gospel to a secularized culture. Sometimes it looks as if now in the way we put the problems we go back behind even the scholastic period to the apologetic theology of the five first centuries. The difference is, however, that the Apologetes knew that they stood against a world with which they had broken and which they now tried to convert, whereas for us the secularized world is our own spiritual climate from which we cannot withdraw. Therefore, we theologians stand under a heavy pressure which in former times did not exist or at any rate did not exist to the present extent. On the one hand we know ourselves bound to the authority of the books of the Bible in which the truth of God is revealed to us in a unique way; on the other hand we are in spite of ourselves bound up with the way of life of our own era. That last fact is not so much a result of conscious conviction as it is of more or less unconscious experience. We are bound to a residuum of semi-scientific convictions, political ideas, and literary and artistic fashions. Of course we may try to withdraw from these "powers of the air," but then we are in danger of getting out of touch with our culture. We consider it, however, as our calling in the interpretation of the gospel to "become all things to all men" (1 Cor. 9:22). We cannot interpret salvation in Christ unless we enter into what I will call in this chapter the "sense of life" of the world around us—which is also our own sense of life.

It has often been said that twentieth-century theology has rediscovered eschatology. That may be too much to say. It is true, however, that we came to exprience the word and the matter of eschatology in new ways. And it is also true that eschatology in the last half century went through a very stirring and rapid history which was also the result of rapid changes in the sense of life and which can be seen as typical for the relation between theology and modern sense of life in general. In what follows we want to draw a schematized sketch of this history. We will limit it mainly to European Protestant theology. Outside these limits we find very interesting developments to which we will refer occasionally, but the traditions inside these limits are dominant in the whole of theology today. Of course the schematic treatment has to deny the smooth transitions which characterize real life and also does injustice to many individual shades. On the other hand this treatment can help people get to know their way in a bewildering multitude of names and titles in which one is in danger of not seeing the woods for the trees. After what has been said at the beginning, it will be clear why we find our starting point in the changing senses of life and then investigate the way in which theology has responded to them.

PREVIOUS HISTORY

One can often read that the new flourishing of eschatology in our century was made possible by the studies of Johannes Weiss and Albert Schweitzer in the eschatology of Jesus. Neither of them, however, drew dogmatic consequences out of their new insights, or if so then only traditional ones. Schweitzer saw the significance of Jesus in the "ethical completion of the world" to which he had devoted his life unsuccessfully and which we, differently from Jesus' conception, anticipate as the result not of a divine intervention but of human effort. So Schweitzer de-eschatologized the message of Jesus. That was why the impetus for an eschatological renewal had to come from somewhere else. It came from the shock caused by the First World War, which put an end to all kinds of security and did so in a radical way that later generations can hardly understand. Until then many had combined an optimistic evolutionist sense of life with a form of Christian faith modeled upon it. Now both members of this combination fell away. In their place came a sense of crisis which could conceive of the Christian faith only as an encounter with the Ultimate, the eschaton. This conception certainly sought support and inspiration in philosophers and theologians of the prewar period but could find it only in individuals who had suffered from life, like Kierkegaard; Blumhardt, father and son; and more recently in the Swiss religious socialists Hermann Kutter and Leonhard Ragaz.

See Johannes Weiss, *Die Predigt Jesu vom Reiche Gottes* (Göttingen, 1893) and Albert Schweitzer, *The Quest of the Historical Jesus,* translated by W. Montgomery (London: A. & C. Black, Ltd., 1922), where one should especially read the famous "final consideration." Schweitzer continued to exercise dogmatic influence mainly through the Swiss school of Martin Werner and his followers Fritz Buri and Ulrich Neuenschwander. In their view historic Christendom is the result of the frustrated expectation of the near coming of the kingdom of God, which started a process of de-eschatologizing by which Christianity became more and more estranged from its nature. It was also in Switzerland that the most pertinent resistance against this view arose, as shown in the relevant writings of Cullmann, Flückiger, Kümmel, and Michaelis.

SENSE OF CRISIS

From now on most theologians can no longer see eternity and time in such a harmony with one another as had been the case in the previous period. God's world is now no longer the core of ours but on the contrary, the judgment upon ours. The most penetrating interrelation between the biblical message and this sense of crisis was laid in the second edition (1921) of Karl Barth's *The Epistle to the Romans*, translated by Edwyn C. Hoskyns (New York: Oxford

University Press, 1933); the first edition of 1918 was still in the line of Ragaz. God's word comes, according to young Barth, "vertically from above," "as lightning" as the "tangent" and the "line of death" to our existence, so that man can meet God only "every now and again" when man is confronted by the eschaton, by the Ultimate. Well-known is the sentence, "If Christianity be not altogether thoroughgoing eschatology, there remains in it no relationship whatever with Christ" (p. 314). This eschatology, however, was not meant in the sense of the classical tradition. God again and again strikes man vertically as lightning. One must not expect him on the horizontal line of our history in either a nearer or more remote future. Such horizontality belongs to our present humanity and its sin and death.

Others tried to combine eschatology and the contemporary sense of crisis in a similar way. Also in 1922 Paul Althaus published the first edition of his *Die letzten Dinge* (Gütersloh: C. Bertelsmann), written against the background of Windelband's philosophy of values. In this book man enters into contact with the Last in his "being touched by transcendent holiness." That reminds us of Barth. But Althaus knows that this value, this "axion" as he calls it, can only be fully experienced through death. Therefore, he acknowledged in the first edition, along with the "axiological" eschatology, a certain room for horizontal, "teleological" eschatology. although this future eschaton remains unrelated to the course of history.

In the same period Paul Tillich, one of the religious socialists, combined eschatology and the sense of crisis in an article "Eschatology and History" (1927). Words like "consummation," "judgment," and "salvation," he argued, do not refer to empirical situations but are symbols for the decision nature of reality; wherever transcendence in judgment, fulfillment, and decision breaks through our closed existence, we experience the Ultimate. For these three and many other theologians this interpretation of eschatology meant a radical demythologizing of biblical presentations, primarily necessary because of the fact that everywhere in the Bible the encounter with the Ultimate comes about not in an existential here-and-now but in a chronological future.

In Barth's *The Epistle to the Romans* one should see especially the explanation of Romans 8:24 f. (pp. 313 ff.) and of 13:11 (pp. 497 f.). The study of Tillich can be found in his volume *The Interpretation of History* (New York/London: Charles Scribner's Sons, 1936), pp. 266-282.

SENSE OF HISTORY

The period of the sense of crisis did not last long. For good reasons we can take the year 1925 as a turning point. Something was changing then. Did the sense of crisis recede? Or did the theologians discover that the biblical message does not respond to it? At any rate in eschatological literature the discovery is evident that essential biblical notions about time and history are neglected if we conceive the Ultimate only as the stroke of the lightning of eternity into the here-and-now of human decision. The Ultimate is as much or even more what will happen in the future. Theology cannot forget this in spite of the widespread fear of getting into the quicksand of historicism.

We can clearly observe the turn in Barth and Althaus. In 1926 Barth published his lecture on 1 Corinthians 15 under the title *Die Auferstehung der Toten* (München: C. Kaiser, 1926). Not less than *The Epistle to the Romans* this work testifies to an actualistic interpretation of eschatology. It is curious now for us to hear that this interpretation was attacked by Rudolf Bultmann, who at that time was Barth's partisan; he agreed with Barth's idea but denied that he had a right to appeal to Paul: "It is after all no small thing when one either through reinterpretation or through critical separation interprets away, so to speak, the whole 'end history,' those thoughts of Paul which in the first place are the clearest and which without doubt were important to him!" Since then, both positions have been reshuffled in a striking way! Now with the help of hermeneutics Bultmann is ready to push aside those thoughts of Paul as unauthentic. Barth to the contrary drew the conclusion that in the choice between the genuine Paul and his own sense of life he had better choose Paul. It was a long time, however, before he gave dogmatic expression to this new conviction. That he did in his magnificent section "The Eternity and Glory of God" in *Church Dogmatics II, 1* (1940), pp. 608-677, where he describes eternity under three aspects: *Vorzeitlichkeit, Überzeitlichkeit, Nachzeitlich-keit*—"the simultaneity of beginning, middle and end" (p. 608). Under the first heading he gave full weight to what Althaus had called the teleological dimension.

Althaus himself went through a similar change in these years. The third edition of *Die letzten Dinge* (Gütersloh: C. Bertelsmann, 1926) was already a revision, and the fourth edition (Gütersloh: C. Bertelsmann, 1933) was rewritten. There the philosophy of values and the term "axiological" disappear. The direction towards the future now plays a dominant role, and the tension between the "already" and the "not yet" is now phrased in more biblical categories.

This sense of history, breaking through in the twenties, received an enormous stimulus from the years of the Second World War, in which history more than before was experienced as being a struggle and as having direction towards the future. This experience had its consequences for eschatology, in which now the teleological dimension almost became the one and all. The book which interpreted this sense of teleology most eloquently for innumerable people was Oscar Cullmann's *Christ and Time* (Philadelphia: The Westminster Press, 1950) with its well-known comparison of the "already" and the "not yet" with D-day and V-day of 1944 and 1945. Stauffer's *New Testament Theology* (London: SCM Press, 1955) had a similar trend and effect. A particular inspiration came from the theme of the second assembly of the World Council of Churches at Evanston: "Christ—the Hope of the World." Thirty-two outstanding theologians wrote the beautiful preparatory report *Christ—the Hope of the World* (1954). In the same period before Evanston some theologians published studies on the theme of eschatology, of which the best known are Paul S. Minear with his *Christian Hope and the Second Coming* (Philadelphia: The Westminster Press, 1954), a book of high value for the understanding of eschatological imagery, Emil Brunner with his noble book *Das Ewige als Zukunft und Gegenwart* (Zürich: Zwingli Verlag, 1953), and the Anglican canon J. E. Fison with *The Christian Hope: The Presence and the Parousia* (London, New York: Longmans, Green, 1954). The latter two titles are characteristic. They prove that the authors do not abandon the eschatological meaning of the here-and-now but to the contrary want to express the unity in tension between the present and the future. As we saw, that held good also for Althaus and Barth. It is not less true of Cullmann with his emphasis on Christ as "the middle of time" as well as of the Evanston report with its "having and hoping." It is a remarkable and felicitous fact that the change in the sense of life did not drive theology from the one extreme to the other.

Bultmann's criticism of Barth's *Die Auferstehung der Toten* was published in 1926 in *Theologische Blätter* and afterwards in *Glauben und Verstehen, Vol. I* (Tübingen: J. C. B. Mohr (Paul Siebeck), 1954), pp. 38-64 (see page 57). Barth's treatment of God's eternity is found in *Church Dogmatics II, 1* (Edinburgh: T. & T. Clark, 1957), pages 608-677. This passage poses an interesting problem of autobiography. Here Barth sees himself as a man who in a former period *(The Epistle to the Romans)* one-sidedly stressed the teleological aspect of eternity! (See pages 634 ff.) The reader notices with amazement that that was what Barth was after! He understands better what follows. "But it is also clear that with all this art and eloquence I missed the distinctive feature of the passage, the teleology which it ascribes to time as it moves towards a real end" (p. 635). It is remarkable and important that Barth rejected the "linear" and therefore one-sidedly teleological concept of Cullmann. More than any other, Barth by his doctrine of the three relations between eternity and time withdrew from the danger of one-sided construction. See also *Church Dogmatics III, 2, §* 47. 1 with an attack on Cullmann.

Althaus' change is partly influenced by the criticism which his fellow Lutherans H. W. Schmidt *(Zeit und Ewigkeit,* Gütersloh: C. Bertelsmann, 1927) and Folke Holmström *(Das eschatologische Denken der Gegenwart,* German edition, Gütersloh: C. Bertelsmann: 1936) passed on him. For quite other reasons Fritz Buri, in the line of Albert Schweitzer, traced the way in which this actualistic eschatology had projected itself onto the New Testament *(Die Bedeutung der neutestamentlichen Eschatologie für die neuere protestantische Theologie,* Zürich & Leipzig: Max Niehans Verlag, 1935).

The teleological approach was also strong in Dutch theology. This was already the case in the short confession issued by the Netherlands Reformed Church under the title *Foundations and Perspectives* (1949); see especially the articles 1 and 8 end, 14 beginning, 17 end, 18 and 29. The same trend is found in G. J.

Heering, *De Verwachting van het koninkrijk Gods* (Arnhem: Van Loghum Slaterus, 1952) and in H. Berkhof, *Christ the Meaning of History* (1958; English edition, Richmond: John Knox Press, 1966).

SENSE OF EXISTENCE

In the years shortly before and after Evanston, in which teleological eschatology bore its ripest fruits, it had already passed its culmination in Germany. There an opposite sense of life had developed which found its most impressive interpreter in Bultmann. It could seem for a moment that now the pendulum swung back to the actualistic eschatology as it existed in the time of the sense of crisis. This was true inasmuch as Bultmann, Tillich, and Gogarten had not participated in the turn towards the teleological perspective mainly from fear of historicism. Each one of them found in his own way a philosophical support in young Heidegger's *Sein und Zeit,* I (1927), published in 1962 as *Being and Time* (London: SCM Press, Ltd.). By and by the sense of crisis receded from their minds. Their theology became less tense but by no means less actualistic. Following Heidegger, Bultmann presupposed that the horizontal dimension of life means *Weltverfallenheit* (being fallen to the world) and that real *Geschichtlichkeit* (historical nature) of our existence comes into being where God through the proclamation of the crucified Christ calls man to his vertical dimension, to the *Eigentlichkeit* (authenticity) of existing, which means at the same time *Entweltlichung* (being withdrawn from the horizontal world).

Probably this perspective had to do with postwar discouragement about the political future of the world. Its background was, however, not less a growing respect for the world which is now of age and which with its science and technics creates a society and a history to which the Christian message is irrelevant. Therefore, Christian faith withdraws into its own unassailable realm, the realm of existence. Of course in this vertical dimension there is no room for a teleological eschatology, related as it is by nature to the horizontality of history. Bultmann does not deny that such eschatology is present almost everywhere in the New Testament, but then, according to him, we have to deal with objectifying mythological forms of what by its nature is a special *Existenzverständnis* (conception of existence).

> "Eschatological preaching views the present time in the light of the future and it says to men that this present world, the world of nature and history, the world in which we live our lives and make our plans is not the only world; that this world is temporal and transitory, yes, ultimately empty and unreal in the face of eternity" (p. 23). "As in the conception of heaven the transcendence of God is imagined by means of the category of space, so in the conception of the end of the world, the idea of the transcendence of God is imagined by means of the category of time" (p. 22). "This then is the deeper meaning of the mythological preaching of Jesus—to be open to God's future which is really imminent for every one of us" (p. 31).

This fact implies for Bultmann a kind of life after death, certainly; but we cannot make any statement about it, lest we incorporate this life against its. nature into the horizontal world of things at our disposal.

Bultmann's quotations are from *Jesus Christ and Mythology* (New York: Charles Scribner's Sons, 1958). One should see particularly the second part, "The Interpretation of Mythological Eschatology," pp. 22-34. Also relevant is the last chapter of *History and Eschatology* (Edinburgh: University Press, 1957) and the clear presentation of Bultmann's eschatology in the last chapter of Walter Schmithals, *Die Theologie Rudolf Bultmanns* (Tübingen: J. C. B. Mohr (Paul Siebeck), 1966). The Neo-Bultmannians, who by their emphasis on the historical Jesus seem to give more room to the dimension of history, nevertheless stick to Bultmann's concept of eschatology. See Gerhard Ebeling, *Das Wesen des christlichen Glaubens* (Tübingen: J. C. B. Mohr (Paul Siebeck), 1959): "The future is that which announces itself to the conscience as yet to come" (p. 240). Faith creates future for itself, also beyond the limits of death. But Ebeling is averse to teleological eschatology which might suggest that faith is "a conglomeration of views of the world which are mythological in nature" (p. 233). Eschatology is the expression of faithful existing which projects itself toward the God who approaches us from out of his future.

A separate position is held by the Swiss theologian Heinrich Ott who, starting in existentialistic categories, wanted to build a bridge toward Barth and who has attempted it in the field of eschatology. Already, in his dissertation *Geschichte und Heilsgeschichte in der Theologie Rudolf Bultmanns* (Tübingen: J. C. B. Mohr (Paul Siebeck), 1955), he refused to consider the teleological element in New Testament eschatology as a mere mythical objectivation, and he asked whether these conceptions did not have an existential meaning beyond that which Bultmann had indicated. The program implied in this question he carried out himself some years later in a small but extremely thoughtful study, "Eschatologie, Versuch eines dogmatischen Grundrisses" in *Theologische Studien*, Heft 53 (Zürich: Evangelischer Verlag AG., Zollikon, 1958). For Ott, far more than for Bultmann, the existential is a category of personal encounter. We live in the "amazement that results from the encounter with the Lord," and therefore eschatology must be displayed "as the expression of the encounter with the Lord as the 'eschaton.'" (p. 5). For Ott eschatological statements are not information about realms of life unknown until now, but consequences for the future drawn from the encounter with God in Christ's cross and resurrection. Unlike Bultmann, Ott sees our being directed towards future as an essential structure of our existential reality. The study proves that Ott has set out on a fruitful third way between existentialism and objectivism. His result is not much different from that of Althaus or Brunner. Within the existentialist movement this study is an exception, however. In the general opinion, the sense of existence and the sense of the future were mutually exclusive.

SENSE OF THE FUTURE

This situation could not last. Around 1960 theological discussions in Germany were swinging back. The eschatological poverty to which theology in the perspective of the sense of existence seemed to be doomed made many doubtful about this perspective itself. No wonder that besides this tradition, the sense of history and the theological method connected with it survived. However, they had a hard fight against the existentialist conception, as can easily be sensed from the cautious and laborious way in which Walter Kreck—in continuous polemic against Bultmann, Gogarten, and others—builds up his concept under the felicitous title *Die Zukunft des Gekommenen* (München: C. Kaiser Verlag, 1961). His own position is near Althaus and Brunner but different from them in that he swims against a heavy stream. Nevertheless, at that moment change was already in the air. Horizontality and teleology were about to resume their rights. No doubt this change was caused by considerations of biblical theology. A special source of inspiration was Old Testament theology as pursued by von Rad and his school. While Bultmann and his school read the New Testament as the witness to an essentially ahistorical existential event, von Rad and his partisans read the Old Testament (and the New Testament as its continuation) as confessions of the deeds of Israel's God in history, deeds in which the individual existence partakes and by which it is referred to the future.

The authority of Scriptures, however, is not the only background of this change; here also the sense of life plays its own role. A younger generation felt that Bultmann's individualism and "neo-pietism" could not inspire the architects of our future nor the fighters against hunger, war, oppression, and discrimination. Has the gospel nothing to contribute to the progress of humanity and to the shaping of the year 2000? Questions like these again put the future-directedness of Christian faith in the center of attention. It was possible to revert to the flourishing of eschatology in its teleological period. This time, however, a much stronger emphasis is laid on the *futurum*, on that which has not yet arrived. To the same extent, the existential and methodological momentum of the "already" receded. Now all history is seen as pointing forward to a future beyond all our horizons.

The first one who dared to make such a sharp turn was Wolfhart Pannenberg. But his starting point is still the concept of history. This concept is now expanded—from Christ as its center, back through Israel, and forward through the alliance of the gospel with the Western mind—to the totality of all human events. In this whole history God is present. But he will not be revealed before the end, when the process of his becoming disclosed will be completed. His total revelation will mean resurrection from the dead. We know this because "Jesus of Nazareth is the end of a not yet completed history and for that reason is its center of meaning which cannot be exhausted by us who are yet on the way." He is that in his destiny and particularly in his resurrection. "The universal revelation of God's deity had not been realized in the history of Israel, but was realized only in the destiny of Jesus of Nazareth, insofar as in this destiny the end of all events has already taken place" (p. 103).

These trends of thought were almost revolutionary. Nevertheless, only a few years later they were surpassed by those of Jürgen Moltmann and Gerhard Sauter, both deeply influenced by the Jewish Marxist philosopher Ernst Bloch. For Moltmann even in the resurrection of Jesus, the Ultimate is not yet realized, either for others or for Jesus himself. His objection to Pannenberg is that the risen Jesus himself would no longer have any future. But even Jesus is *vorläufig*, which means both "provisional" and "forerunner"; all God's saving acts are signposts towards a mere future coming of God. We live by the *promissio*, which means both "promise" and "being sent to the front." Faith is hope.

Sauter writes in the same spirit. He finds in Pannenberg still too much continuity between our history and the eschaton; only the future will reveal what relation God in his faithfulness has established with our present. Jesus is the one who "sets our way toward the future" (p. 274), who "verifies the promise, makes it true, brings it to realization in the anticipatory vision of its fulfillment" (p. 258). Moltmann and Sauter think from an unknown future towards its anticipating signs in history (under the influence of Bloch and with an appeal to Romans 4:17b, 8:24 and 2 Corinthians 5:7), not the other way round. Therefore, they "know" much less about the eschaton than those like Althaus, Brunner, Ott, and Kreck, who go in the other direction. That is why they hardly fill this expectation with any real content. Even so, however, they made it possible for many to discover convergent lines between the gospel and their own futuristic sense of life as people of the second half of the twentieth century. But these thinkers do not want to suggest anything more than convergence. They see our modern futurism as an extrapolation of technical and social developments, whereas God's future is a *novum* which has only a contingent relation to our historical evolutions. Moltmann distinguishes sharply between *futurum* (a word cognate to the Greek *phuo* which means "to grow") and *adventus.* Where this distinction is not made, the result is a futuristic eschatology. In that direction Harvey Cox moves in *The Secular City* (New York: The Macmillan Company, 1965) where he basically identifies the kingdom of God with the developing urban society and its anonymity and mobility, its liberty and equality. In that case eschatology becomes a mere immanent reality.

Wolfhart Pannenberg first came to the fore with his concept in "Heilsgeschehen und Geschichte," in *Kerygma und Dogma* Vol. V (1959), pp. 218-237, 259-288. The first quotation is from that article (p. 287). He gave a broader display in the symposium which he edited, *Offenbarung als Geschichte* (Götingen: Vandenhoeck & Ruprecht, 1961), in which are of particular interest his "Dogmatische Thesen zur Lehre von der Offenbarung" (pp. 91-114); the second quotation is borrowed from point 4 of these theses.

In this new development Ernst Bloch occupies a place which can be compared with that of Heidegger in the theology of existence. That is mainly due to his substantial and impressive principal work *Das Prinzip Hoffnung* (Wissenschaftliche Ausgabe, 3 Vols. (Frankfurt a. M.: Suhrkamp Verlag, 1967). For Bloch man is a "utopian" being. The concept of God by Moses and the eschatological attitude of Jesus are expressions of this utopian sense of life, which in recent centuries had expressed itself more and more in humanistic and atheistic categories.

Moltmann sprang into fame with his *Theology of Hope* (New York: Harper & Row, Publishers, 1967). His method was mainly criticized by adherents of a teleological eschatology who preferred to think from the center in Christ towards the future and not the other way round. Moltmann defended his method on the one hand and gave more room to the opposite approach on the other hand, as seen in the collection *Diskussion über die "Theologie der Hoffnung,"* Wolf-Dieter Marsch, ed. (München: C. Kaiser Verlag, 1967).

Walter Kreck in the second edition of his *Die Zukunft des Gekommenen* (München: C. Kaiser Verlag, 1966) gives an interesting appendix (pp. 199 ff.) where he deals with the concepts of Pannenberg, Moltmann, Cullmann, and others.

In 1965 Gerhard Sauter published *Zukunft und Verheissung. Das Problem der Zukunft in der gegenwärtigen theologischen und philosophischen Diskussion* (Zürich: Zwingli Verlag). The two quotations are borrowed from pages 274 and 258. The similarities between Moltmann and Sauter, who wrote their books at the same time without knowing each other's work, are striking. Against that background the differences are also notable; they are concerned with the relationships between philosophy and theology; Moltmann has a higher appreciation of the first in relation to the second than Sauter has. See the Moltmann collection *Diskussion*, mentioned previously. For his distinction between *futurum* and *adventus* see pages 210 ff. Moltmann sees as the main question at stake: "Does the present decide the future in extrapolations or does the future decide the present in anticipations?" (p. 209).

SENSE OF EVOLUTION

The sense of partaking in a great evolutionary process within an unlimited space and time comes home more and more also to those who have hardly any idea of its scientific grounds. Often this sense is combined, as far as possible, with the sense of existence, and it allies itself very easily with the sense of future. But nowhere in contemporary Protestant thought did it become until now so dominant that it led to its own project of eschatology. This situation is somewhat different from that in Anglican theology and much different from that in Roman Catholic theology. Of course the first name which here comes to mind is that of the Jesuit and biologist Pierre Teilhard de Chardin in his impressive endeavor to demonstrate the convergence of Christian faith and biological theory of evolution. In that perspective he also developed in a natural manner thoughts about eschatology. The world of human mind, the so-called "noosphere," develops into ever greater personalization, fullness of love ("amorization") and of community ("socialization"). Love drives the individual minds to larger and larger unities. One day this process will reach its critical point of "maturation and escape," when the mind like a ripe fruit will fall from the material and organic tree of this planet. Then a tremendous urge will arise to escape from the earth. This urge will divide: A part of mankind will want to escape in order to dominate the world from outside better than before; another part will desire to see the world die and to become absorbed into God. So Teilhard does not expect the salvation of all: The "materialized spirit" will experience eternal perdition; the "spiritualized matter," eternal fellowship. The goal of the world will be attained by those in whom the perfectly "amorized" mind dissociates itself from matter and shifts its center of gravity to the point towards which the whole process of evolution is pulled —"God-Omega." This looks like pantheism, but on the contrary it is the acme of personalization. It looks extremely spiritual, and truly so, because the earth and its corporality will be thrown off like the run-out stage of a rocket. It may be due also to this last feature that until now Teilhard's eschatology has not had much influence.

The famous Catholic theologian Karl Rahner is inspired by Teilhard de Chardin; he develops his theology within the pattern of an evolutionary world concept. But his eschatology is also inspired by other viewpoints. For him an eschatological statement is only tenable as that "which can be said on the basis of the presence of the realized eschaton, that is, Christ." For according to Rahner we must say that "even the eschatological statements of Scripture are not, and are not intended to be anything but statements of Christology and anthropology related to the mode of their fulfillment." This method reminds us of Ott and of the teleological eschatologists from Althaus to Kreck. Rahner sees his way to build upon this method a project which in its main lines keeps within the framework of classical eschatology. As a matter of fact, so does Teilhard de Chardin. For both the central evolutionary aspect is given by the reality of the God-man Jesus Christ, who is the first fruits of that perfect unity with God towards which the world of mankind in its evolution is directed.

For Teilhard see the end of his principal work *The Phenomenon of Man*, translated by Bernard Wall (New York: Harper & Row, Publishers, 1959), especially IV and III. 3 "The End." See also the end of *The Future of Man*, translated by Norman Denny (New York: Harper & Row, Publishers, 1964).
For Karl Rahner see "Theologische Prinzipien der Hermeneutik eschatologischer Aussagen," in *Schriften zur Theologie* IV (Cologne: Benziger & Co. AG, 1960), pp. 401–428 (the quotations are from pages 417 and 428), and "Die Christologie innerhalb einer evolutiven Weltanschauung," *Schriften zur Theologie* V, (Cologne: Benziger & Co. AG, 1962), pp. 183–221.
A most pronounced evolutionary theologian is the Dutch father A. Hulsbosch. See his book *De Schepping Gods* (Roermond en

Maaseik: J. J. Romen & Zonen, 1963); and for his evolutionary Christology see his article in the Dutch *Tijdschrift voor Theologie* VI, 3 (1966), pp. 250–273: "Jezus Christus, gekend als mens, beleden als Zoon Gods."

FINAL CONSIDERATIONS

Probably the reader is confused by the multitude of viewpoints. In that case I would remind him of what was said before—that theology has to interpret the biblical truth to generations who think in quite different categories. That does not necessarily mean weakening or disturbing the biblical message, because it expresses not a timeless truth, but truth as encounter. That is why even as early as New Testament times eschatological statements differed as widely as, for example, those in Revelation and those in the first Epistle of John. Therefore, we are not afraid of quite different interpretations. They can have a complementary relationship, and in their togetherness they can reflect the inexhaustible truth which even together they can no more than approximate.

As we said, they can have a complementary relation. It is not necessarily so. We can also imagine interpretations in which what was meant in the biblical message no longer comes through effectively. As an example of this in the eschatological field, there are the statements of the existentialist theology, insofar as it expresses only the here-and-now and leaves no room for hope as future-directedness. On no point should the idea of complementarity seduce us to the neutrality of a mere observer. That would mean the end of theology. We will have to ask what projects are better or worse, and why; and how we ourselves in our situation can interpret Christian expectation even better. Some of the concepts mentioned before give me the impression of being worse than others because they seem to suffer from a feeling of inferiority and nervousness in respect of "man of today," "modern thinking," etc. Such feelings foster the inclination to jump quickly upon the triumphal car of some present-day philosopher or fashionable trend of thinking in the hope of making Christian profits out of their successes. The punishment of this attitude is that together with this car one will soon be laid aside and so will do more harm than good to the cause which he wants to serve. A theologian must have a far stronger belief in the message which he hears in the Bible than in the dominant contemporary views of life (which indeed never succeeded one another so quickly as today). He cannot expect more from these views than that they will expose one element of the truth and will offer one small approach, *methodos*, to the world of God's redemption. No wonder that so many studies do not go much beyond an eschatological methodology and do not really lay hold on the content. We should not forget the sober classical wisdom, "The choice of a method is open" (*Methodus est arbitraria*).

The ones least affected by this criticism are the theologians mentioned under the heading "Sense of History." Their heyday (from the end of the War until Evanston) was the richest period in eschatology of our century. The category of history is more fruitful and more comprehensive than the other ones. It can include also the categories of existence, future, and evolution, whereas an inclusion the other way round is either impossible or very tortuous. And without this pattern of salvation-history, existence becomes ghostly, evolution deterministic, and the future utopian.

It is impossible, however, to stop in the concept of history of the aforementioned period. This concept must indeed, far more deliberately than could happen in that period, assimilate the other notions involved. In view of the concept of existence this means that we must base our eschatology not only upon Christology but on pneumatology—the Spirit within us is also a first fruits of the future —and in connection with pneumatology also upon anthropology. In view of the sense of future this means that we must enter deeper into the relation between the Future and the future, between the Christian expectation and the expectations which at the moment are being projected along the way of extrapolation—which implies that we will have to reconsider the classical doctrine of "the signs of the time." Finally in view of the sense of evolution this means that more than before we will have to make the connection of the narrow line of God's revealing history with world history in general and in a retrospective view also with the evolutionary history of nature. The Bible in both its parts takes the lead on this point: The God of redemption is the God of the whole of history and also the

God of nature. From the center of salvation he is confessed as omnipresent. By his redemptive deeds he builds the teleological bridge between the beginning and the end.

What is expressed in these last sentences finds a broad elaboration in the World Council Study Paper *God in Nature and History* (Faith and Order Studies 1964–1967), the promising result of a wide theological cooperation.

Notes

I. The Crisis of the Christian Expectation of the Future

1. One may object that in verse 28 the writer suddenly speaks entirely in futuristic terms. According to Bultmann, however, this verse is an addition made by a redactor in order to bring the passage into agreement with the common belief of the church. In Paul, Bultmann sees time and again, especially in 1 Corinthians 15, a backsliding into abandoned "objectivistic" conceptions.

2. Later on Moltmann emphasized also the other direction: We only know about God's future because God's deeds in past and present lay the foundation for such an expectation. See Chapter XIII of this book.

II. The Method of the Christian Expectation of the Future

1. See also Isaiah 4:5; 10:24–27;811:16; 48:20 f.; 52:11 f.

2. Th. C. Vriezen, *An Outline of Old Testament Theology* (Oxford: Basil Blackwell, 1958), p. 355.

3. "First fruits" (*aparchè*) applied to Christ: 1 Cor. 15:20; to the Spirit: Rom. 8:23; the Spirit as "guarantee" (*arrabon*): 2 Cor. 1:22; Eph. 1:14.

4. Other passages which express this Christological foundation are Romans 14:9, 1 Corinthians 6:14, 2 Corinthians 4:14, 1 Thessalonians 4:14 and 5:10.

5. A similar foundation of hope on what we experience already now in grace and comfort, peace and joy, we find in Romans 15:13 and 2 Thessalonians 2:16 and in a slightly different way in Romans 8:23, where the very having of the Spirit as first fruits makes us groan as we wait for the full gift, "the adoption as sons" and "the redemption of our bodies" (i.e., of our total existence).

6. A combination of Christological and pneumatological foundation is also found in Romans 8:11.

7. Having put this first, we can subsequently convert the thesis as Moltmann does and say that Christ and the Spirit are meant as signposts to the unknown future of God. If, however, we put that viewpoint first, eschatology is in danger of losing its content and becoming limited to hope as a formal principle.

8. Joel 2: present fulfillment in Acts 2, future fulfillment in Rev. 9; Zech. 12:10: present fulfillment in John 19:37, future in Matt. 24:30 and Rev. 1:7; Mal. 3:1 f.: present fulfillment in Mark 1:2, future in Rev. 6:17.

9. See Romans 5:1–5, 1 Corinthians 13:13, Galatians 5:5 f., Ephesians 1:15–18, Colossians 1:3–5, 1 Thessalonians 1:3.

10. *The Heidelberg Catechism* (Philadelphia, Boston: United Church Press, 1962), p. 60.

11. This distorted conception of Christian hope as a mere compensation for the pains of this life can rather easily appeal to those classical theologians, like Augustine and Calvin, who had a strong eschatological outlook. For Calvin see his famous chapter in the *Institutes* "On the Meditation of Future Life" (Bk. III, Ch. 9) which begins with the characteristic sentence: "Whatever kind of tribulation presses upon us, we must ever look to this end: to accustom ourselves to contempt for the present life and to be aroused thereby to meditate upon the future life." (*Institutes of the Christian Religion*, Vol. 1, edited by John T. McNeill, Philadelphia: The Westminster Press, 1960.)

III. THE LANGUAGE OF THE CHRISTIAN EXPECTATION OF THE FUTURE

1. The best book I know about biblical imagery is Paul S. Minear, *Christian Hope and the Second Coming* (Philadelphia: The Westminster Press, 1954), especially Part II, with chapters on the clouds of heaven, the thief, the dragon, the earthquake, the keys of heaven, and the trumpet. For the trumpet see Numbers 10:1–10, Joshua 6, Judges 7, 1 Kings 1:32 ff., 2 Kings 11:12 ff., 2 Chronicles 5,12 ff., Ezekiel 33: 1–6, Joel 2:1–3 and 15–29, Amos 3:6, Zephaniah 1:14 ff., 1 Corinthians 15:51 f., 1 Thessalonians 4:16, Revelation 8 and 9. For more examples, see also the article *salpingx* in *Theologisches Wörterbuch zum Neuen Testament*, Gerhard Kittel, editor (Stuttgart: W. Kohlhammer, 1933).

2. See Exodus 13: 21 f. and 19:16, Psalm 97:2, Ezekiel 1:4, Daniel 7:13, Mark 9:7, Acts 1:9. More examples are mentioned in *Theologisches Wörterbuch zum Neuen Testament*, the article *nephelè.*

IV. TIME AND ETERNITY

1. Paul Althaus, *Die letzten Dinge*, 5th ed. (Gütersloh: C. Bertelsmann, 1949), p. 251.

2. Subtitle: *The Primitive Christian Conception of Time and History*, translated by Floyd V. Filson (Philadelphia: The Westminster Press, 1950).

3. See James Barr, *Biblical Words for Time* (London: SCM Press, 1962), which contains a continuous polemic with Cullmann.

4. See Matthew 24, Mark 13, Luke 21, 1 Corinthians 15, 23–30, Thessalonians 2, Revelation 18–22.

5. See Matthew 22:30, 1 Corinthians 15:50, 1 Corinthians 6:13.

6. The most satisfactory presentation of the relation between time and eternity, I found in Karl Barth, *Church Dogmatics*, I, 2, § 14.1 and III, 2, § 47. The reader can find another treatment of this problem from my hand in *Christ the Meaning of History* (Richmond: John Knox Press, 1966), pp. 184 ff.

7. Resurrection is central in 1 Corinthians 15; the second coming, in Mark 13 and 2 Thessalonians 2; the last judgment in Matthew 13 and 25; eternal life, in the closing chapters of Revelation.

V. THE FUTURE AS RESURRECTION

1. See Isaiah 25–27, particularly Daniel 12:1–3, likely also Psalms 16,

49, 73. Was this belief of Israel due to influence from outside? Many think of the religion of Zoroaster, as mediated in the time of Persian dominance. We have no certainty about it. The question is only of minor interest because Israel's faith, following a deep intuition, repelled or accepted foreign elements according as they lay or did not lie in the perspective of its own nature.

2. Acts 4:2. See also Romans 5:10, 8:29, 14:9; 1 Corinthians 6:14; 2 Corinthians 4:14; Colossians 1:18; 1 Thessalonians 4:14; Revelation 1:5; and, of course, the whole trend of 1 Corinthians 15.

3. See John 3:5 and 6:63, Romans 6:4 and 8:10, 1 Corinthians 15:45, 2 Corinthians 3:6 and 5:17, Titus 3:5.

4. Rom. 8:11, 1 Peter 1:3.

5. See Romans 6:11, 2 Corinthians 4:10, Galatians 2:20, Ephesians 2:1–5, Colossians 2:12.

6. The words in Ephesians 5:14 "arise from the dead" are not the author's own words but probably a quotation from an early Christian hymn.

7. 1 Peter 1:3.

8. Rom. 8:23.

9. 2 Tim. 2:18. Also in the proto-Pauline epistles the rising with Christ is predominantly seen as future: Romans 6:5, 8 and 8:8, 1 Corinthians 15:12 ff., Philippians 3:10 f.

10. Mark 16:12.

11. 1 Cor. 15:44.

12. 1 Cor. 15:50.

13. 1 Cor. 15:44–49.

VI. The Future as Second Coming

1. The parousia element is but weakly represented in most recent studies on eschatology. An exception is canon J. E. Fison, *The Christian Hope: The Presence and the Parousia* (London, New York: Longmans, Green, 1954). His stressing of the parousia is a consequence of his personalistic approach of eschatology "real life is meeting" (p. 44). God's love as revealed in Christ calls for a final reunion. He characterizes the parousia with Shakespeare's word: "Journeys end in lovers meeting" (p. 46).

2. See John 14:3; cf. Acts 1:11 and Hebrews 9:28.

3. Schlatter and Büchsel are in favor of the first solution; Calvin, Bultmann and Dodd, the second; Zahn, the third; Barrett and Grosheide, all three together.

4. See Matthew 24:43 f., Luke 12:39 f., 1 Thessalonians 5:1–5, 2 Peter 3:10, Revelation 3:3 and 16:15.

5. Compare with 1 Thessalonians 5:11 and 2 Thessalonians 2:1–10, where the idea of a soon and sudden return is opposed by the argument that the development towards that event is yet incomplete.

6. Rev. 1:7.

7. Col. 3:4.

8. 1 Thess. 4:17.

9. Rev. 19:14, which in my opinion has to be seen together with 17, 14, and 20:4.

10. Rom. 8:19–23.

11. For the whole of this subject I refer to Barth, *Church Dogmatics* IV, 3, § 69.4 where he develops illuminating thoughts both about the connection among resurrection, outpouring of the Spirit, and parousia; and about the unity between Christ and his redeemed humanity.

VII. THE FUTURE AS JUDGMENT

1. The famous hymn *Dies irae dies illa*, probably made by Thomas of Celano (about 1240 A.D). Palestrina, Haydn, Mozart, Cherubini, and Verdi wrote music to it.

2. John 3:17. See also 3:18 and 5:24.

3. Ps. 75:7.

4. Isa. 11:4.

5. For example, Luke 2:34 f. and John 9:39 f.

6. Luke 1:51 ff.

7. See 1 Corinthians 11:28 and 31, 2 Corinthians 13:5, 1 Thessalonians 2:3–6, 1 Peter 4:17.

8. 2 Cor. 5:10.

9. See Romans 2:6; 1 Corinthians 3:8, 13 and 4:5; 2 Corinthians 5:10; Galatians 6:7 ff.; Colossians 3:23 f.; 1 Peter 1:17; Matthew 25.

10. Rom. 2:12–16, cf. Matt. 25:31–46, but this last passage views particularly those deeds in which non-Christians show mercy to persecuted Christians.

11. Friedrich Zündel: *Johann Christoph Blumhardt*, 10th ed. (Giessen: Brunnen-Verlag, 1926), p. 392.

VIII. THE FUTURE AS SEPARATION

1. In most handbooks the theme of hell is only superficially touched —somewhat deeper by Althaus and Brunner. It speaks volumes that in the great theological encyclopedia *Die Religion in Geschichte und Gegenwart*, third edition, Kurt Galling, editor, (Tübingen: Mohr, 1957), at variance of the rules, no dogmatical treatment of hell is found.

2. In *De Spectaculis*, closing chapter (see *The Anti-Nicene Fathers*, Vol. III, Roberts and Donaldson, editors, New York: Charles Scribner's Sons, 1925). For Nietzsche in his *The Genealogy of Morals* this was a splendid proof for his thesis that Christian ethics are a product of resentment (see *The Complete Works of Friedrich Neitzsche*, V. 13, Dr. Oscar Levy, editor, Edinburgh and London: T. N. Foulis, 1909–1913).

3. The King James Version and other older translations created confusion because they translated with "hell" not only *gehenna* but also the Hebrew *sheol* and the Greek *hades*, which point to a subterranean dwelling place for the ghosts of the dead. So it seemed that the Old Testament knew also about hell. Newer translations render *sheol/hades* as "realm of the dead" or "Hades."

4. C. S. Lewis, *The Great Divorce* (New York: The Macmillan Company, 1946).

5. See Matthew 11:21 ff. and Luke 12:47 ff.

6. To discover the difference in the conception of hell between the New Testament and the contemporary Jewish Apocalyptic, see Ethiopic

Enoch 27:90–104, Slavonic Enoch 10:40–42, Assumptio Mosis 10:10, Syriac Baruch 59:7–12 and 85:12 f. The hell conceptions of this literature found their way into Christendom mainly through the so-called Apocalypse of Peter (first half of second century A.D.), which surpasses all its predecessors by its detailed picture of hell (see Ethiopian text chapters 7–12, Egyptian text chapters 21–33) and became a source of inspiration for later Christian art and imagination, e.g., Dante's *Inferno*.

7. 2 Cor. 2:16.
8. We find this tendency deeply founded and eloquently expressed in Barth, especially in *Church Dogmatics* II, 1, § 30.2, the end. Hell has to function in preaching in this way indeed, but not only in this way.
9. Heb. 2:3.
10. Mark 9:48, a quotation from Isa. 66:24 in an altered and deepened meaning.

IX. THE FUTURE AS GLORIFICATION

1. See John 1:14, 5:26, 11:25, 14:6; 1 John 1:1 f., 5:20; Romans 5:10; Colossians 3:14.
2. See John 3:36, 5:24, 6:40 and 47, 17:3, 20:31, 1 John 3:14, 5:12; Romans 6:4, 8:6 and 10; 2 Corinthians 4:10; Colossians 3:3.
3. 1 Cor. 15:19.
4. For examples, see Romans 8:18 and 21, 1 Corinthians 2:7 and 15:43, 2 Corinthians 3:7–11 and 18, Colossians 1:27 and 3:4, 2 Timothy 2:10, Hebrews 2:10, 1 Peter 4:13 and 1 Peter 5, and especially the Gospel of John. See the article *doxa* in *Theologisches Wörterbuch zum Neuen Testament*.
5. Exod. 33:18–23.
6. 2 Cor. 3:18. The verb *katoptrizo* means both "look into a mirror" and "mirror" ("reflect").
7. 2 Peter 1:4.
8. See Exodus 33:18–23, Psalm 27, Matthew 5:8, 1 Corinthians 12:12, 2 Corinthians 3:18, Hebrews 12:14, 1 John 3:2, Revelation 22:4.
9. Kenneth E. Kirk, bishop of Oxford, delivered the Bampton Lectures of 1928 on this subject. I used the abridged edition, *The Vision of God: The Christian Doctrine of the Summum Bonum* (London, New York: Longmans, Green and Co., 1931).
10. Heb. 3 and 4, especially 4:8–11; cf. Rev. 14:13.
11. Luke 19:11–27. We think also of the expressions about a future reigning with Christ (2 Tim. 2:12) and a serving of God day and night in his temple (Rev. 7:15).
12. See Revelation 21:24 f., 22:1 f., and 5b.

X. THE DOUBLE IMAGE OF THE FUTURE

1. Rev. 20:10, 2 Thess. 1:9.
2. Matt. 25:41 and 46; cf. 24:51 and 25:30.
3. The quoted texts are 1 Corinthians 15:22, 1 Timothy 2:3 f. and 4:10, 1 John 2:1 f. See also Romans 11:25 and 30–32 and 36, 1 Corinthians 15:28, Ephesians 1:10, Philippians 2:11. To this group belongs also Romans 5:12–21, where in the verses 15 and 19 "the many" (Greek: *hoi polloi*)

means "all" as is evident from the context in 15 and 18. The reason for this usage is explained in *Theologisches Wörterbuch zum Neuen Testament*, the article *polloi*. Both King James Version and Revised Standard Version wrongly translate "many." (Are they afraid to suggest the salvation of all men?); New English Bible has "so many" (vs. 15) and "the many" (vs. 19).

4. The distinction between these two perspectives is best expressed by Althaus and also expressed well by Brunner.

5. Mark 13:32.

6. It is not by chance that 1 Corinthians 15 with its "universalistic" tendency (see vss. 22 and 28) expresses this concern explicitly: "Otherwise, what do people mean by being baptized on behalf of the dead?" (vs. 29).

7. Rom. 11:32.

8. Many recent European writers on this subject are rather near to this conception—Althaus, Brunner, Kreck, and particularly Barth (e.g., *Church Dogmatics*, IV, 3, § 70.3, last pages)—but they all hesitate to make the final step. Many Anglo-Saxon authors do not hesitate to make this step, but they are often more interested in psychological arguments than in exegetical difficulties. For example, see John Baillie, *And the Life Everlasting* (New York: Charles Scribner's Sons, 1933), pp. 236–243. The noblest example of this mentality I find in the last chapter of F. D. Maurice, *Theological Essays* (New York: Harper & Brothers, Publishers, 1957), in the words, "I am obliged to believe in an abyss of love which is deeper than the abyss of death: I dare not lose faith in that love" (p. 323).

9. James 1:18. The same idea is found in Romans 8:19–22, where "the creation" not only includes what we call "nature" but also non-believing humanity in its groaning and longing.

XI. The Future and Our Death

1. See John 12:24, Mark 8:35, Philippians 2:9. For the glorification on the cross see John 12:23 ff., 13:31 f., 17:1; cf. Hebrews 2:10 and 5:9.

2. See Romans 6:1–11, 7:4 and 6, 8:13 and 17; 2 Corinthians 4:7–12, 6:8–10; Galatians 6:14; Philippians 3:10. One should also notice the ambiguity in John 12:24, which refers not only to Christ but also to men and insofar is meant as an exhortation (see 25 f.).

3. See Matthew 27:52; John 11:11; Acts 7:60; 1 Corinthians 11:30, 15:6, 18, 20, and 51; 1 Thessalonians 4:13–15.

4. Heb. 12:22 f. Other passages to which the traditional conception of the intermediary state appeals, are the parable of the Rich Man and Lazarus, Jesus' promise to the criminal on the cross, the words in John 14:2 f. about the many rooms in the house of the Father.

5. 1 Cor. 15:53.

6. Traditional Roman Catholic theology wrongly appealed to 1 Corinthians 3:15. Several theologians infer from the remarkable passages 1 Peter 3:18–20 and 4:6 general possibilities of conversion and spiritual growth beyond the limit of death; that is, however, more than is said by the writer himself.

7. Rev. 6:9–11.

8. Luke 23:43, 2 Cor. 5:8, Phil. 1:23, 1 Thess. 4:14 and 17; cf. John 14:2 f. and 17:24; Rev. 14:13.

9. *Institutes of the Christian Religion*, Vol. 2, Bk. III, Sect. XXV. 6, John T. McNeill, ed. (Philadelphia: The Westminster Press, 1960), p. 998.

XII. Eschatology and Futurology

1. Karl Barth, *The Epistle to the Romans*, translated by Edwyn C. Hoskyns (New York: Oxford University Press, 1933), p. 314.
2. Friedrich Nietzsche, "Sprüche und Sentenzen," I, 2, in *Werke XII* (Leipzig: Alfred Kröner Verlag, 1919), p. 239.